Academic Challenges In Reading

Academic Challenges In Reading

Helen Taylor Abdulaziz

Alfred D. Stover

Center for English as a Second Language
University of Arizona

Illustrations by
Patricia Eisenberg

REGENTS/PRENTICE HALL
Englewood Cliffs, New Jersey 07632

LIBRARY OF CONGRESS
Library of Congress Cataloging-in-Publication Data

Abdulaziz, Helen Taylor.
Academic challenges in reading / Helen Taylor Abdulaziz, Alfred D. Stover ; illustrations by Patricia Eisenberg.
p. cm.
Includes index.
ISBN 0-13-000811-7
1. English language--Textbooks for foreign speakers. 2. College readers. I. Stover, Alfred D. II. Title.
PE1128.A24 1989
428.6'4--dc19 88-7273
CIP

Editorial/production supervision and
interior design: Jan Stephan
Cover design: Baldino Design
Manufacturing buyer: Peter Havens and Art Michalez

Printed in the United States of America

10 9 8 7 6 5 4

ISBN 0-13-000811-7

Prentice-Hall International (UK) Limited, *London*
Prentice-Hall of Australia Pty. Limited, *Sydney*
Prentice-Hall Canada Inc., *Toronto*
Prentice-Hall Hispanoamericana, S.A., *Mexico*
Prentice-Hall of India Private Limited, *New Delhi*
Prentice-Hall of Japan, Inc., *Tokyo*
Simon & Schuster Asia Pte. Ltd., *Singapore*
Editora Prentice-Hall do Brasil, Ltda., *Rio de Janeiro*

To Our Families

Mohyeddin, Hana, Mona
Henrietta, Lacey, Daryn Amanda
Edna Arnett
Helen and Perry Taylor
and
in Memory of
Henry E. Arnett

Contents

Preface

Academic Challenges in Reading, a beginning reader, is an English for specific-purposes text designed to meet the needs of the low-level ESL student. The text is based on three major ideas.

1. Reading skills can be practiced at the lowest levels of language instruction.
2. Students at low levels of English language study need more extensive specific-purpose reading experience than is currently available in other materials for this level. Therefore, the readings in this text may be longer than in other texts. These readings will encourage students to read faster while improving their comprehension. The lessons focus on the kinds of reading skills necessary for university success, while providing all the benefits of specific-purpose materials. However, students should follow up these materials with more sophisticated reading courses which further develop their skills.
3. Students will be more motivated to read if they view the material as being important or useful in their careers. The topics are from a variety of scientific and business areas and are especially beneficial to those who plan to pursue careers in those fields. Many students will know these concepts in their native language, and these materials will exploit this knowledge by helping students to associate it to new English language experiences, thereby increasing comprehension and maximizing skill development. Some lessons, such as those on the stock market and the Emancipation Proclamation, may introduce materials with which students are unfamiliar. In these cases, the "preview" should explain the content sufficiently for students to read with comprehension.

The text includes thirty-five lessons in five chapters: math, science, business, social science and charts and graphs. The text has been developed for a target group of low-level students who have been exposed to, but do not necessarily have control of, the four simple verb tenses, present and past passive tenses, high-frequency models, such as can, will, should and must, and certain elementary adverbial clauses of time and condition. Although the topics may seem technical, the majority of the vocabulary used to define and explain them is in everyday English. Technical vocabulary words (that is, scientific or business jargon) have been carefully defined in context, and students are not expected to memorize them.

The grammar in the early lessons is somewhat controlled. For example, in the chapter on math, the familiar first or second person is often used to avoid the passive. Passive and other complex grammatical structures are used after the second chapter (science).

The math chapter is first because it requires the lowest level of language skill. However, it is assumed that students understand addition and subtraction. The three middle units may introduce new concepts, but the language has been simplified so that beginning students can learn new facts. It is possible to go from Chapter 1 to Chapter 2, 3, or 4 depending on the interest of the class. The last chapter, reading charts and graphs, has been written at a higher level of language and so should be done after students have had some experience with this textbook and developed some reading skills. Depending on the level of the class, the charts may be interspersed in the readings that are related by content in the business and social science units. A section called "Reading Graphs" has been included at the end of lessons in which the content of the sample graph fits. The teacher can elect to read the graphs either with these lessons or at the end of the book.

Part of the aim of the extensive-reading exercises is to help students read faster with better comprehension. The number of words in each reading appears at the end of each reading so that students can calculate their reading speed. It is strongly recommended that students keep the Personal Performance Charts found in lesson 35. Keeping careful records of their time and comprehension scores allows students to see areas that are weak and in need of improvement. These charts can be used for self-assessment in the final lesson.

Each reading contains exercises to assist in the development of reading skills. Reading rate, main idea, and comprehension questions accompany readings. Other exercises occur throughout the book.

Initially, students may have difficulty with the kind of deductive learning expected of them because students at this level typically enter instruction with low levels of vocabulary and comprehension. For this reason, explanations have been kept to a minimum. It is suggested that as students complete the exercises, instructors provide them positive reinforcement and well thought-out hints and prompts.

Preview Each reading is preceded by a "preview" which helps students to recall knowledge they probably already have about a topic or to prime them for new material. All readings are accompanied by illustrations or photographs to assist in the previewing process. Students should be encouraged to preview the lessons and to examine the illustrations before reading.

Words per Minute As students finish, their words per minute (wpm) should be calculated individually and entered on their Personal Progress Charts in lesson 35.

> To calculate the words per minute, divide the number of words in each selection by the number of minutes it took the student to read the selection. A more accurate and preferable method is to change minutes and seconds to seconds. Divide the number of words by the total number of seconds, and multiply this figure by 60. For example, if it took a student four minutes and 30 seconds to read a selection of 500 words, divide 500 by 270 seconds (four minutes times 60 seconds plus 30 seconds). $500/270 = 1.85$. Multiply 1.85 by 60 to give the wpm. $1.85 \times 60 = 111$ wpm.

It is advisable to keep the wpm as accurately as possible. After the first several readings, students can perform their own calculations and keep their own charts.

Main Idea A multiple-choice main idea exercise follows each reading. Students are required to distinguish a statement of the main idea from other statements that are true about the reading. In several lessons, the multiple-choice problem is followed by an exercise that requires students to identify the main subdivisions of the article. For a true test of comprehension, students should not refer to the reading to complete the main idea exercise.

Comprehension Questions The comprehension questions are meant to test students' understanding. The questions quiz students on the main idea, their understanding of the vocabulary, and on implications they draw from the reading. The latter questions are marked with an asterisk *. Students should not refer to the reading to answer the questions the first time. After correcting the comprehension questions and entering their score on the Personal Progress Charts in lesson 35, students should be encouraged to correct their answers by looking in the text. They are also required to write the line numbers for the sentences in the article that state the main idea and to support their answers to the inference questions.

Using New Vocabulary Questions on new vocabulary words are intended to lead the student through the reading idea by idea and new word by new word. For students who score well on comprehension, these questions may be redundant. A score of 70 percent is considered sufficient comprehension. Students surpassing this level can proceed to the next exercise. Students failing to meet it should do the "Using New Vocabulary" exercise, or they should return to the text to answer the missed questions.

Vocabulary in Context In this exercise, students must identify the meanings of words based on context clues. Sufficient clues exist for the beginning student.

Roots and Affixes and Word Forms These exercises serve primarily to introduce the concept of word families to help students figure out new words by examining roots and affixes and to help them begin to acquire word-building skills.

Problems to Solve One of the most difficult things to understand in a second language is word problems. Several problems of this type are included in the math-oriented lessons to give students the opportunity for practice. Students and teachers will find that the math and logic of the problems are not difficult; the difficulty lies in understanding the language needed to solve the problems. The word problems are designed to help the student through the process of understanding and solving word problems.

Grammar Exercises A variety of grammar exercises are given in the text. These include exercises on cloze, pronoun reference, passive, and subject-verb identification. The cloze exercises serve as a test of both vocabulary and grammar clues, which are important reading skills. Beginning in the third chapter, the passive is used in the readings and is dealt with in exercises to illustrate the notions of action and doer of the action. The treatment of the passive grammatically is not included. Explicit grammar explanations are best left to other types of textbooks. Our goal here is to aid students in recognizing and understanding the grammar necessary for reading comprehension. Similarly, exercises on pronoun reference have been introduced in the third unit because this skill is a necessary and important one for readers of all levels. A final type of grammar exercise is one in which students must identify the subject and verb in long, more complex sentences.

Additional Reading This reading usually includes only one quick exercise to test comprehension. It is not a timed reading and is not meant for extensive analysis.

Discussion Questions These questions are for classes or students who have a further interest in the subject.

SUGGESTED TEACHING STRATEGY

Day One (50-minute period)

1. Preview the lesson with the class according to the instructions for each lesson.
2. Time-read the lessons, even if you don't plan to calculate words per minute and keep records. Timed reading encourages students to read through the article without stopping to ask a lot of questions and losing their train of thought. Students should read as fast as possible, with understanding, but without using a dictionary. As they finish, their words per minute can be calculated and entered on their Personal Progress Charts in lesson 35.
3. Do the main idea and comprehension test without looking back to the text for help.
4. Correct the comprehension questions. At first, this is best done as a class discussion so that the teacher can point out why errors were made. Under teacher supervision, students can identify the main idea statement and support their inferences. As students become more skilled in these areas, they may be individually corrected and allowed to continue through the lesson at their own pace.
5. Assign skills exercises for classwork and homework as time permits.

Day Two

6. Collect or go over exercise as needed. If time permits, preview or read the next article.

Instructors who want additional readings on these topics or related topics are encouraged to check books out from the juvenile sections of municipal, college, and university libraries.

The authors wish to acknowledge those individuals who assisted with this project. First, David Chisholm, Dean Jensen, Christine Gorder, and Mohyeddin Abdulaziz assisted with language translations needed in chapter 3. Second, Pat Eisenberg, our artist, not only provided wonderful illustrations but in most cases was responsible for the idea and creation of the illustration. Finally, we would like to acknowledge the students whose comments and questions helped greatly during the field testing of this material.

HTA
ADS

chapter

1

Math

lesson
1

Numbers

preview Talking about numbers is often necessary. All languages use numbers. Learning a new language means learning new words for numbers. In this lesson, you will read about numbers, number systems, and different kinds of numbers.

1 one

2 two

3 three

4 four

5 five

6 six

7 seven

8 eight

9 nine

There are different number systems. For example, computers use the *binary system.* This system uses the base two, and it has only two numbers: zero and one. Another number system is the *octal system.* This system uses the base eight. There are eight numbers in this system: zero, one, two, three, four, five, six, and seven. A third system is the *decimal system.* This system uses the base ten and has ten numbers: zero, one, two, three, four, five, six, seven, eight, and nine. The word "decimal" comes from the Latin word *decem. Decem* means "ten." The decimal system is very common. The American money system uses the decimal system ($1.62).

In the decimal system, numbers such as six hundred and eighty one, fourteen, or three are *whole numbers* or *integers.* The number three (3) is a one-*digit* number and it has one place. The number fourteen (14) has two digits or two places. The number six hundred and eighty-one (681) has three digits or three places. Each digit has a name.

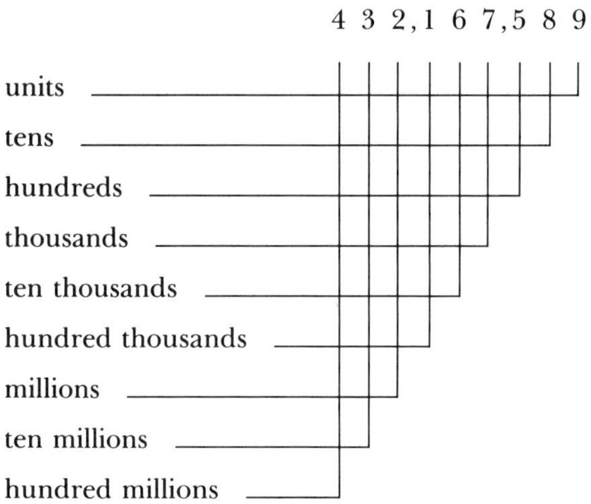

Therefore, you should say a number such as 7,681,239 like this: seven million, six hundred and eighty-one thousand, two hundred and thirty-nine. Americans usually write a comma (,) between every three digits.

Whole numbers or integers are either positive or negative. Four, ten, eighty-nine, and four hundred and thirty-eight are *positive* numbers. Negative numbers have a minus (−) sign in front of them. Minus four (−4,), −10, −32, and −212 are *negative* numbers.

People sometimes talk about even and odd numbers. Two, four, and six are examples of *even* numbers. Three, five, and seven are examples of *odd* numbers.

268 words ________ time ________ wpm

COMPREHENSION QUESTIONS

Write **T** before true statements; true statements are correct. Write **F** before false statements; false statements are not correct. Inferences are marked with an asterisk (*). Use the information from the article, but do not look back at the reading.

_______ 1. There are many different number systems.

_______ 2. The decimal system uses base ten.

_______ 3. Computers use the decimal system.

_______ 4. The number 4,675 has three digits.

_______ 5. *Any number can be a base.

_______ 6. *Decem* means "eight" in Latin.

_______ 7. Eighteen is a whole number.

_______ 8. Minus sixteen is a positive number.

_______ 9. A minus sign goes with negative numbers.

_______ 10. Read 167,562 like this: one hundred and sixty-seven thousand, five hundred and sixty-two.

_______ 11. Americans use a comma (,) between every four digits.

_______ 12. *Fifteen is an odd number.

_______ number answered correctly

USING NEW VOCABULARY

Do this exercise if your score on the comprehension questions was under 9 or if you want more practice with new vocabulary. Did you understand the new words? Read the article again. Look at the new words. Answer these questions. *Do not* use your dictionary.

1. What base does the binary system use?
2. How many numbers are in the binary system?
3. What base does the octal system use?
4. How many numbers are in the octal system?
5. What base does the decimal system use?
6. Where does the word "decimal" come from?

7. What does "decimal" mean?
8. Give an example of a whole number.
9. Are *whole numbers* and *integers* the same?
10. How many places does a three-digit number have?
11. Give an example of a five-digit number.
12. How many digits are in this number? 37,465,813
13. Write commas in this number. 416047893
14. What is a negative number?
15. Is this number positive or negative? −15
16. Give four examples of even numbers.
17. Count from 50 to 76 by even numbers.
18. Count from 15 to 37 by odd numbers.

PRACTICE READING NUMBERS

Read these numbers aloud in English.

1. 4,276	5. 98	9. 504
2. 7,864,314	6. 68,453,180	10. 453,678,111
3. 32,459	7. 322,678	11. 420,068
4. 50,007	8. 19	12. 316

PREFIXES AND ROOTS

Many English words come from Latin and Greek words. Latin was the language of ancient Rome. Greek is the language of modern and ancient Greece. Greek and Latin roots are parts of some English words. A *root* is part of a word. A *prefix* is at the beginning of the word. If students learn roots and prefixes, they can learn many English words. Look at these prefixes and learn their meanings.

uni	one
bi	two
tri	three
oct	eight
dec	ten
cent	one hundred
mille	one thousand

Look at these words from the lesson and their meanings.

unit	one of something
binary	a number system with only two numbers
octal	a number system with eight numbers
decimal	a number system with ten numbers

Read these sentences and answer the questions that follow each sentence.

1. Bicycles and tricycles are both vehicles. Very young children learn to ride tricycles, and older children begin to ride bicycles. How many wheels does a tricycle have? ________ How many wheels does a bicycle have? ________
2. A triangle is a geometric shape. How many angles does it have? ________
3. The octopus lives in the ocean. It has many legs. How many legs does it have? ________
4. Nurses, police officers, and fire fighters usually wear uniforms. Are all nurses' uniforms similar or different? ________
5. The Vietnam War lasted for more than a decade. How many years is a decade? ________
6. The Moors stayed in Spain for more than six centuries. How many years is a century? ________

lesson 2

Basic Operations

preview You are probably familiar with using numbers to add, subtract, multiply, and divide in your language. These operations are the same in English. In this article you will learn how to read the problems in English.

$$4 + 3 = 7$$

$$7 - 3 = 4$$

$$\begin{array}{r} 4 \\ +\,3 \\ \hline 7 \end{array} \qquad \begin{array}{r} 7 \\ -\,4 \\ \hline 3 \end{array}$$

$$4 \times 3 = 12$$

$$4 \cdot 3 = 12$$

$$4 * 3 = 12$$

$$(4)(3) = 12$$

$$\frac{6}{3} = 2$$

$$6 \div 3 = 2$$

$$6/3 = 2$$

There are four basic operations to do with numbers: addition (+), subtraction (−), multiplication (×), and division (÷).

We write *addition* problems with a *plus* sign: $4 + 3 = 7$, and we say, "Four plus three equals seven." We can also say, "Four and three are seven." Seven is the result of four plus three. We call the result of addition the *sum*, so we can say, "The sum of four and three is seven."

We write *subtraction* problems with a *minus* sign: $4 - 3 = 1$, and we say, "Four minus three is one." We can also say, "Three from four equals one." We call the result of a subtraction problem the *difference*, so we can say, "The difference between four and three is one."

We write *multiplication* problems in different ways: $4 \times 3 = 12$ or $4 \cdot 3 = 12$ or $4 * 3 = 12$ or $(4)(3) = 12$ or $xy = 12$. We can read these like this: "For times three is twelve," or "Four threes are twelve." We call the result of multiplication the *product*. We say, "The product of four and three is twelve."

We write *division* problems in different ways, too: $6 \div 3 = 2$ or $6/3 = 2$ or $3\overline{)\,6} = 2$. We can say, "Six divided by three is two," or "Three into six equals two," or "Three goes into six two times." We call the result of division the *quotient*. Sometimes, a number does not divide evenly into another number. In this case there is a *remainder*. For example, seven divided by two equals three, with a remainder of one.

Odd numbers (3, 5, 7 . . .) have a remainder of 1 when we divide them by 2. Two divides into even numbers (2, 4, 6 . . .) equally and does not have a remainder.

The four basic operations in mathematics are addition, subtraction, multiplication, and division. We use these four operations every day when we go shopping, cook dinner, or work around the house.

337 words ________ time ________ wpm

MAIN IDEA

The main idea is the one most important idea in a reading. Choose one main idea for this reading.

a. Four plus three is seven.

b. You can divide even numbers by two.

c. There are four basic operations in mathematics.

d. We can write multiplication problems in different ways.

COMPREHENSION QUESTIONS

Write **T** before true statements; true statements are correct. Write **F** before false statements; false statements are not correct. Inferences are marked with an asterisk (*). Use the information from the article, but *do not* look back at the reading.

_______ 1. The sum of five and two is three.

_______ 2. The difference between eleven and seven is four.

_______ 3. The product of six and six is twelve.

_______ 4. The quotient of six and six is one.

_______ 5. Four times five is twenty.

_______ 6. Three divided by two has a remainder of one.

_______ 7. Nine is an even number.

_______ 8. These symbols mean multiplication: * ×

_______ 9. This is a minus sign: +

_______ 10. *There are only four basic operations in math.

_______ number answered correctly

Write the line number of the sentence that states the main idea of this article. _________

Write the line number of the sentence or sentences that support your answer to question 10. _________

USING NEW VOCABULARY

Do this exercise if your score on the comprehension questions was under 7 or if you want more practice with the new words. Did you understand the new words? Read the article again. Look at the new words. Answer these questions. Do not use your dictionary.

1. What are four basic operations in mathematics?
2. What do you call this sign? +
3. What is the result of 4 + 3?

4. What is the sum of 4 + 3?
5. Are the result and the sum the same?
6. What do you call this sign? −
7. What is the result of 4 − 3?
8. What do you call the result of subtraction?
9. What is the product?
10. What is the quotient?
11. Does a number always divide into another number evenly?
12. Does two go into 7 evenly? 7 ÷ 2
13. Can we divide odd numbers evenly by two?
14. Can we divide even numbers evenly by two?

PROBLEMS TO SOLVE

Read these problems carefully and find the answer. Many math problems are difficult to understand because of the language. These problems will help you read and understand word problems in math.

1. Most states in the United States have sales tax. You must pay sales tax when you buy something. In Tucson, Arizona, the sales tax is 6% (percent). How much sales tax do you pay when you buy a radio for $50? Hint: 6% = .06.
   a. Will the answer be in dollars or percentage?
   b. What operation (+, −, ×, or ÷) will you use to find the answer?
   c. What is the answer?
2. In the last election, Mr. Smith received 43,798 votes. He received 2,375 more votes than Mr. Howard. How many people voted in the election? This problem has two parts.
   a. How many votes did Mr. Howard receive?
   b. What operation did you use to find Mr. Howard's votes?
   c. What operation will you use to find the total votes?
   d. How many people voted?
3. This room is fifteen feet wide by twenty-five feet long. What is the area? Hint: *Area* equals the *length* by the *width*. (A = lw)
   a. Will the answer be in feet or square feet?

b. Which two numbers will you multiply?
c. What is the answer?

4. This semester I bought three English books for class. The first cost $12.95. The second cost $8.95, and the third cost $24.49. What is the total cost of the three books?
   a. What operation should you use?
   b. What is the answer?
   c. If sales tax is 5% (percent) (.05), what will be the total cost, including tax?
   d. What operations did you use to find the answer to 4(c)?
5. I gave the bookstore a one hundred dollar bill for the books I bought for my English class in problem 4. How much change did I get?
   a. What operation will you use?
   b. Which answer from number 4 will you use? b or c?
   c. How much change did I get?
6. J. C. Penney had a good "two-for-one" sale last week. If you bought one pair of shoes, you got a second pair free. I bought two pairs of $25.00 shoes. Shirts were on sale for $9.99 each. I bought three. How much money did I spend?
   a. How many pairs of shoes did I buy?
   b. How much did I pay for all the shoes?
   c. How many shirts did I buy?
   d. How much did I pay for all the shirts?
   e. How much money did I spend before tax?
7. In North America, it is the custom to leave an amount of money to help pay for the service of certain workers such as waitresses, waiters, and taxi drivers. This money is called a tip or gratuity. Most people tip between 15 and 20 percent of the cost of the food. Last weekend the Taylors celebrated their wedding anniversary by going to dinner in a fine restaurant. Their meal cost $60 plus tax. They wanted to leave a 15 percent tip. How much should they leave?
   a. Do you add, subtract, multiply, or divide?
   b. Do you multiply by .15 or by 15?
   c. How much money should they leave for the waiter?

lesson
3

Fractions and Decimals

preview Fractions and decimals are important parts of math. One-half (1/2) and one-fourth (1/4) are fractions. They are often used to measure things in cooking, sewing, and carpentry. Examples of decimals are .25 or .5. Decimals are often used with money. It is important to use the decimal point when you write checks. In English, which of these two numbers is correct: $7.48 or $7,48?

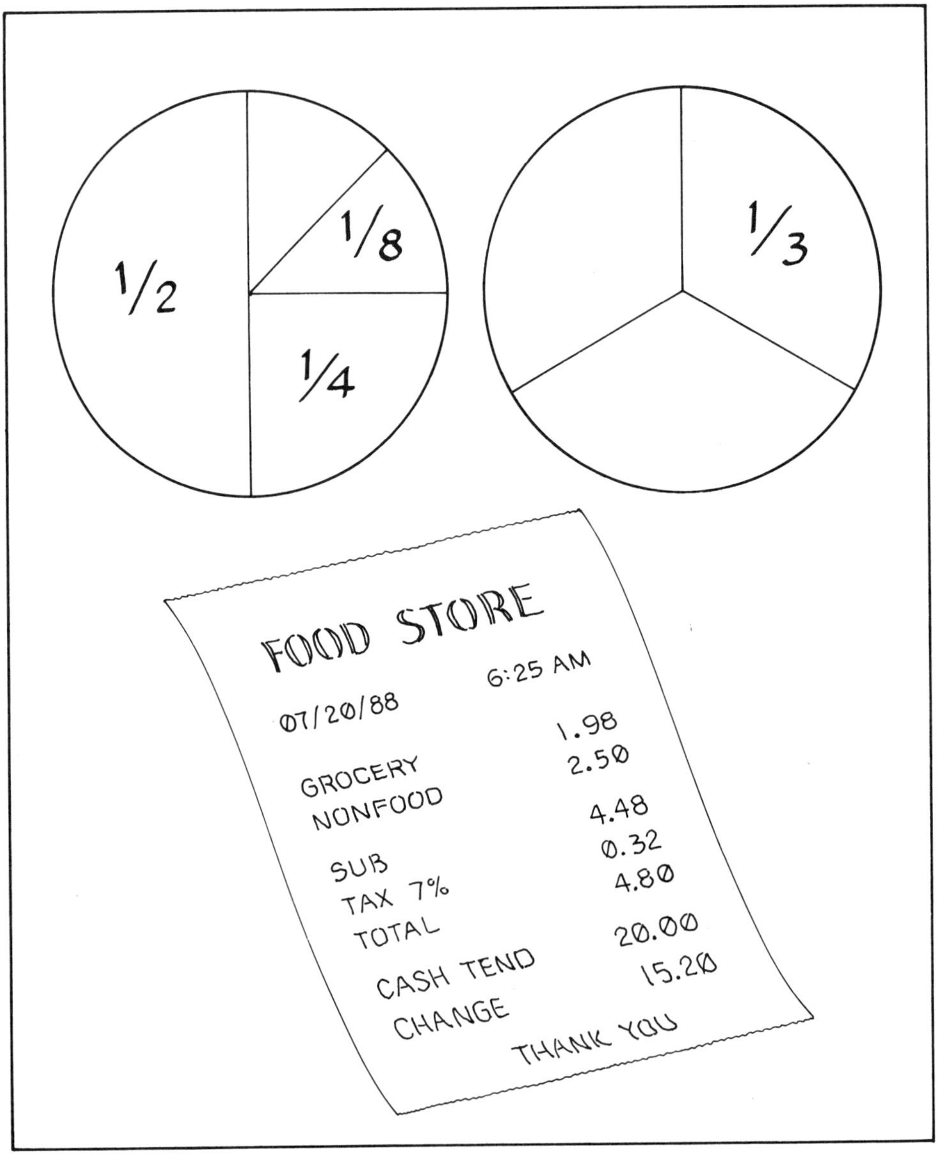

Fractions and decimals are important parts of math. We use words like "half" and "quarter" every day. In fact, we call the 25¢ coin a quarter. Fractions are often used to measure things in cooking, sewing, and carpentry. Decimals are often used with money. It is important to use the decimal point when you write checks. Decimals and fractions are important parts of math that every person uses every day.

A *fraction* is one way of writing a division problem. Three-fourths means three divided by four: 3/4 or 3 ÷ 4. All fractions have two parts. In the fraction a/b, *a* is the *numerator*, and *b* is the *denominator*. When we read a fraction, we add *th* to the denominator. For example, we say "one-fourth" for 1/4, and "one-twelfth" for 1/12, and "seven-sixteenths" for 7/16. But, for 1/2 we say "one-half," and for 2/3 we say "two-thirds."

Two fractions with the same value are equivalent. One-fifth is equivalent to five twenty-fifths, which is equivalent to twenty-hundredths (1/5 = 5/25 = 20/100). One-fifth is a *simplified* fraction.

We can do the four mathematical operations with fractions, too. Before you can add and subtract fractions, you must make all the denominators the same. If all the fractions have the same denominator, you can add and subtract them.

To multiply or divide two fractions, the denominators do not have to be the same. To multiply fractions, you can simply multiply the two denominators and the two numerators. To divide fractions, you must first invert the denominator of one fraction by turning it over. After that, you can multiply the two fractions.

Decimals are another way to write fractions. Many fractions such as one-fourth or four-fifths have exact decimal equivalents: 1/4 = .25 and 4/5 = .8. However, not all fractions have exact decimal equivalents. For example, one-third (1/3) equals .33333. . . .

Decimal numbers have *decimal points* (.). The names of the places, or digits, to the right of the decimal point are similar to the names of the digits on the left of the decimal point, but like fractions, they have *th* at the end. Look at the names below.

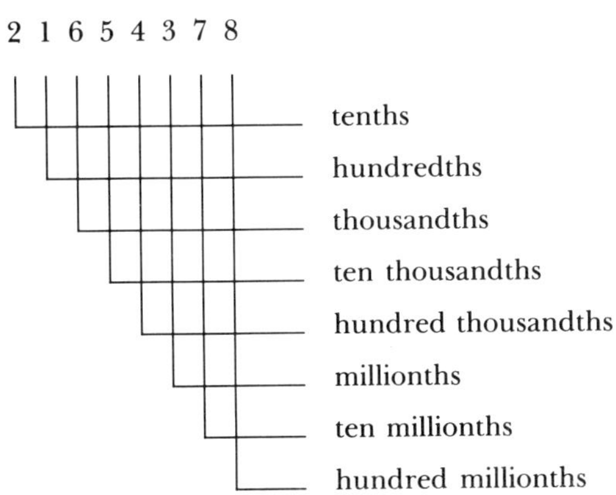

We read .4 as four-tenths and .06 as six-hundredths. Four-tenths is a one-place decimal, and six hundredths is a two-place decimal. The number .138752 is a six-place decimal. We usually read long decimal numbers like this: "point one three eight seven five two."

Decimal numbers sometimes have many places. It is often necessary to shorten them. To make a decimal number short, you may *round it off*. For example, round off .78 to .8 or round off .72 to .7 or round off .75 to .8, but round off .65 to .6.

Decimal numbers are easy to add, subtract, multiply, and divide. To add and subtract decimals, it is not necessary to think about the denominator. You can add, subtract, and multiply decimals the same as whole numbers, but be careful of the decimal point!

In summary, a fraction is a part of a whole number. It is another way of writing a division problem. Decimals are another way to write fractions. Decimal numbers use a decimal point. Decimal numbers are sometimes easier than fractions. Fractions and decimals are like integers because they are negative and positive, and you can do the four basic mathematical operations with them. Both decimals and fractions are basic to mathematics, but we use them every day at the bank, at the grocery store, at work, and at home and when we shop, cook or build something.

613 words ________ time ________ wpm

MAIN IDEA

All of these statements are true, but one is more important than the others. It is the main idea of the reading. Choose the main idea for this article.

a. Fractions are division problems.

b. Decimals and fractions are really not the same thing.

c. Decimals are another way to write fractions.

d. Decimals and fractions are basic to math and everyday life.

COMPREHENSION QUESTIONS

Write **T** before true statements; true statements are correct. Write **F** before false statements; false statements are not correct. Inferences are marked with an asterisk (*). Use the information in the article, but *do not* look back at the reading.

______ 1. One-half and a quarter are decimals.

______ 2. The numerator of 9/10 is 10.

______ 3. "Three-eighths" is one way of saying "three divided by eight."

______ 4. Two examples of equivalent fractions are 5/20 and 1/4.

______ 5. To add or subtract fractions, the denominators must be the same.

______ 6. *If a fraction of the people like the president, then all the people like the president.

______ 7. Decimals are one way of writing fractions.

______ 8. The fraction 1/3 does not have an exact decimal equivalent.

______ 9. The number .216543 has seven digits.

______ 10. The number 642.369 is the same as 642,369.

______ 11. You say .04 like this: four-tenths.

______ 12. If you round off .054, you get .05.

______ 13. *Decimals are easier to add and subtract than fractions.

______ 14. *A decimal with three places is more exact than a decimal with two places.

______ number answered correctly

Write the line number of the sentence that states the main idea of this article. ______

Write the line number of the sentence or sentences that support your answer to questions 6 ______, 13 ______, and 14 ______.

USING NEW VOCABULARY

Do this exercise if your score on the comprehension questions was below 11 or if you want more practice with new words. Did you understand the new words? Read the article again. Look at the new words. Answer these questions. Do not use your dictionary.

1. What do you call the top part of a fraction?
2. What is the denominator?
3. Use numerals to write these fractions:
   seven-eighths
   one-third
   three-sixteenths
4. What are equivalent fractions?
5. What is a simplified fraction?
6. If the teacher simplifies the exercise, does she make it easier or more difficult?
7. What must you do before you can add or subtract fractions?
8. Can you add fractions with different denominators?
9. Can you multiply fractions with different denominators?
10. What must you do before you can divide fractions?
11. What does "invert" mean?
12. The student did only a fraction of the work. Did he do a lot of the work or a little of the work?
13. What is the exact decimal equivalent of 1/4?
14. Does 1/3 have an exact decimal equivalent?
15. How do we say .7?
16. How many places are there in this decimal? .4658
17. How do we usually read this number? .34859120
18. Why do we round off decimals?
19. Why are decimal numbers easy to add and subtract?
20. Is it easier to add decimals or fractions?
21. How do you add, subtract, multiply, and divide decimals?
22. When you multiply decimals, what do you need to be careful of?

VOCABULARY IN CONTEXT

Look at these words in the reading. The line number is in parentheses. Read the sentences. Find the meaning of the word in the text. Do not use your dictionary. Match the new words with the meaning.

______	1. positive (49)	a.	to turn over
______	2. negative (49)	b.	to make a decimal shorter
______	3. equivalent (13)	c.	+
______	4. simplified (15)	d.	–
______	5. round off (38)	e.	the same, equal
______	6. invert (23)	f.	small, easy
______	7. decimal point (29)	g.	

ROOTS AND PREFIXES

Here are some more roots. Learn these roots and their meanings.

equi	equal, the same
vert	turn
a	away
in	in, inside
multi	many

Look at these words from the lesson and their meanings.

equivalent	two things that are the same
invert	to turn something upside down
multiply	to increase in number

Read these sentences and answer the questions that follow.

1. If a equals b, do a and b have the same value?
2. $4y * 2 = 8$ is an equation. Do the two sides have the same value? ________
3. The driver averted his eyes from the terrible automobile accident. Did he look at the accident? ________
4. To convert kilos to pounds, multiply the number of kilos by 2.2. What does "convert" mean? ________

5. Ten, fifteen, and twenty are multiples of five. Is nine a multiple of three? ________
6. A Swiss army knife has multiple uses. Do people use it only as a knife? ________

PROBLEMS TO SOLVE

Read these problems carefully and find the answers. Many math problems are difficult to understand because of the language. These problems will help you read and understand word problems in math.

1. The population of Tucson is 800,000. Fifty thousand people have no cars. What fraction of the population has no car?
   a. What is the numerator?
   b. What is the denominator?
   c. How do you simplify the fraction?
   d. What is the answer?
2. In a large school district there are forty thousand students. Five thousand students are black. Three thousand are Hispanic, and two thousand are other minorities from Asia. What fraction of the students are a minority?
   a. How many minority students are there?
   b. What is the numerator?
   c. What is the denominator?
   d. What is the answer?
3. There are twelve students in an English class. Ten students are from Lebanon. One student is from Saudi Arabia, and one student is from Korea. What fraction of the students are *not* from Lebanon?
   a. What is the numerator?
   b. What is the denominator?
   c. What is the answer?
4. An American family earns $1,500.00 a month. They spend six hundred dollars for their house, four hundred dollars for food, and two hundred dollars for their car payment. What fraction of their money is spent on food and housing?
   a. How much do food and housing cost?
   b. Is the answer to (a) the numerator or the denominator?
   c. What is the answer?

5. Last year, a family's income was \$36,000. They paid \$6,000 to the government. What fraction of their income was paid to the government?
   a. What is the numerator?
   b. What is the denominator?
   c. What is the answer?
6. Normal body temperature is 98.6°F. How much above normal is a body temperature of 101.3°F?
   a. What operation will you use to solve this problem?
   b. What is the answer?
7. The odometer in a car shows the number of miles the car has gone. The odometer reading on the car was 15,476.3 miles. I drove to Phoenix and back. The odometer reading when I got home was 15,716.7 How far did I drive?
   a. What operation will you use?
   b. What is the answer?
8. One student in this class is 168 cm tall. How tall is the student in inches? (1 inch = 2.54 cm.) Change your answer to feet and inches. (12 inches = 1 foot.)
   a. Will you multiply or divide 168 by 2.54?
   b. How tall is the student in inches?
   c. How will you convert inches to feet and inches?
   d. What is your answer?
9. The same student weighs 63 kilos. How many pounds does the student weigh? (1 kilo = 2.2 lb.)
   a. Will you multiply or divide 63 by 2.2?
   b. What is your answer?

lesson 4

Geometry

preview Look around the room. What flat geometric shapes can you identify? What solid shapes can you identify? This article will identify and define some geometric shapes.

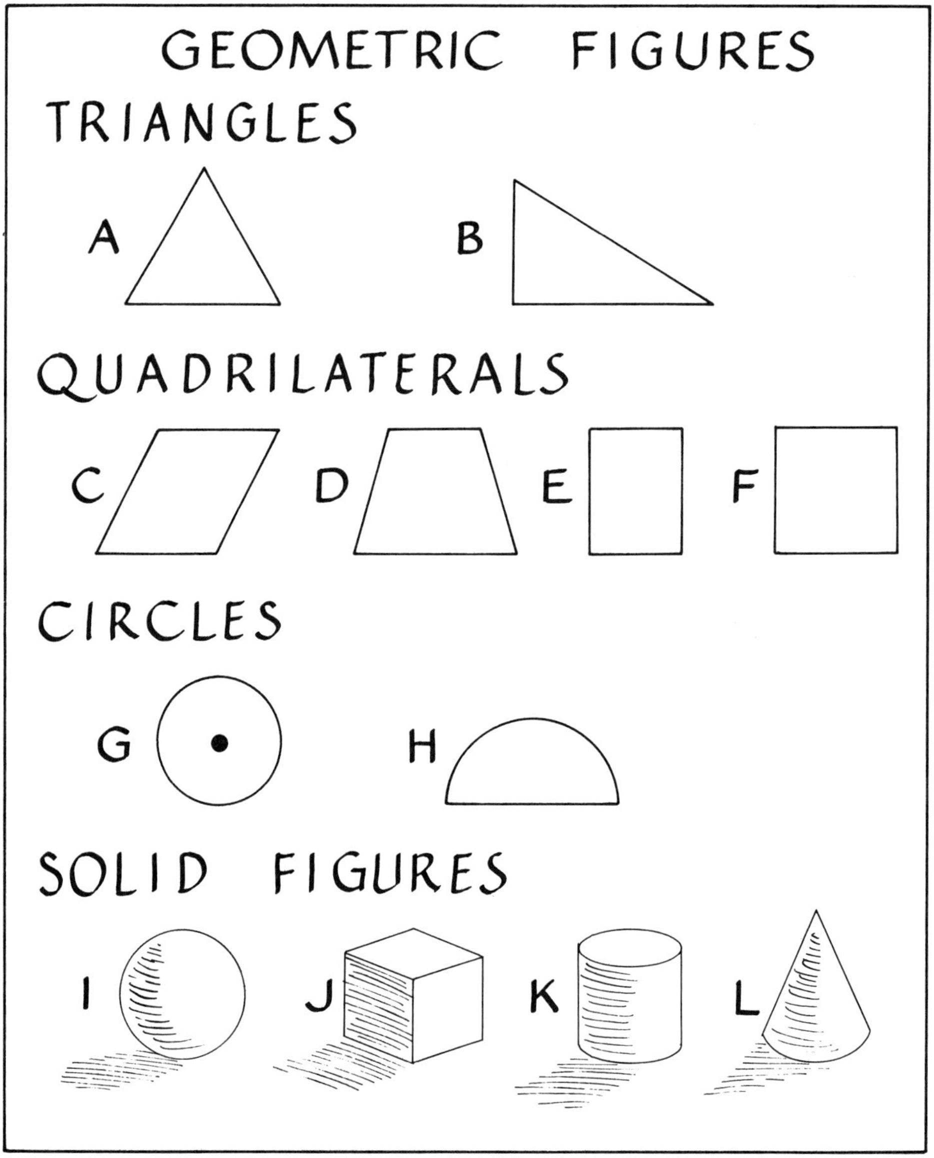

There are two kinds of geometry. Plane geometry is about shapes and figures in a plane, and solid geometry is about solid shapes.

Plane geometry is about shapes in a plane. A plane is a flat surface. It has only length and width. The top of a table is a plane surface.

There are many kinds of plane shapes. One very important shape is a *triangle*. A triangle is a shape that has three sides. Look at Figures A and B. These are triangles. Each triangle has three straight sides and three angles. When two lines come together, or intersect, they make an *angle*. If all three sides of a triangle are the same length, then the triangle is an *equilateral* triangle. The three sides are equal. Figure A is an equilateral triangle. If one of the angles of a triangle is ninety degrees, then the triangle is a *right triangle*. Figure B is a right triangle.

Another kind of geometric shape has four sides. A figure with four sides is a *quadrilateral*. Figures C, D, E, and F are quadrilaterals. Each quadrilateral has a special name. Look at Figure C. In Figure C, the opposite sides are parallel. Parallel lines do not cross or meet. Figure C is a parallelogram. Figure D has only two parallel sides. The name for Figure D is *trapezoid*. Figure E is a parallelogram, but it has a special name because each angle in Figure E is ninety degrees. It is a *rectangle*. A parallelogram with four equal sides and four ninety-degree angles is a *square*, Figure F.

Figure G is a *circle*. Point X is the center of the circle. All points on the circle are the same distance from the center. They are *equidistant* from the center. A straight line from the center (X) of the circle to the outside of the circle is the *radius*. A straight line going through the center of the circle is a *diameter*. Figure H is one-half of a circle. This is a *semicircle*.

Another kind of geometry is *solid geometry*. Solid geometry is about figures that have height, width, and depth. Examples of solid figures are Figures I, J, K, and L. Figure I is a *sphere*. A sphere is like a ball. Figure J is a *cube*. Each side of a cube is a square, and there are six sides. Figure K is a *cylinder*. A cylinder is the shape of a can of food in the supermarket. Figure L is a *cone*. This is the same shape as an ice cream cone.

Plane geometry and solid geometry are two kinds of geometry. Plane geometry is about figures in a flat surface. Solid geometry is about solid shapes. Plane and solid shapes are all around.

463 words ________ time ________ wpm

MAIN IDEA

Choose one main idea for this article about geometry. The other sentences may be true, but one sentence is more important than the others.

a. Two kinds of geometry are about flat and solid figures.

b. An equilateral triangle has three equal sides.

c. Solid geometry is about figures that have height, width, and depth.

d. Parallel lines do not cross or meet.

COMPREHENSION QUESTIONS

Write **T** for each true statement. Write **F** for each false statement. Inferences are marked with an asterisk (*). Use the information in the article, but do not look back at the article. You may look at the illustrations.

_______ 1. Solid geometry is about flat surfaces.

_______ 2. A triangle has three sides and three angles.

_______ 3. The sides of an equilateral triangle are not the same.

_______ 4. A triangle is a quadrilateral.

_______ 5. There are different kinds of quadrilaterals.

_______ 6. Two parallel lines never meet.

_______ 7. A square is a quadrilateral because it has four sides.

_______ 8. A square and a rectangle are always the same.

_______ 9. A square is also a parallelogram.

_______ 10. *In a circle, the radius is one-half the diameter.

_______ 11. A sphere has the same shape as a ball.

_______ 12. *If Figure H is a semicircle, then "semi" probably means one-fourth.

_______ number answered correctly

After correcting your answers, go back to the article and find out the reason for the correct answer. Try to understand the new words from the context.

Write the line number of the sentence that states the main idea of this article. _________

Write the line number of the sentence or sentences that support your answers to questions 10 _________ and 12 _________.

VOCABULARY IN CONTEXT

Read the following sentences. Choose the correct meaning of the underlined word. Use the information in the sentences to find the meaning.

1. If all three sides of a triangle are the same length, the triangle is an *equilateral* triangle.
   a. all sides are different
   b. two sides are equal
   c. all sides are equal
2. A *sphere* is like a ball. It is ________.
   a. round
   b. flat
   c. square
3. A straight line from the center of a circle to the outside is the *radius*. Which is the radius below?
   a. line *AB*
   b. line *DF*
   c. line *XY*

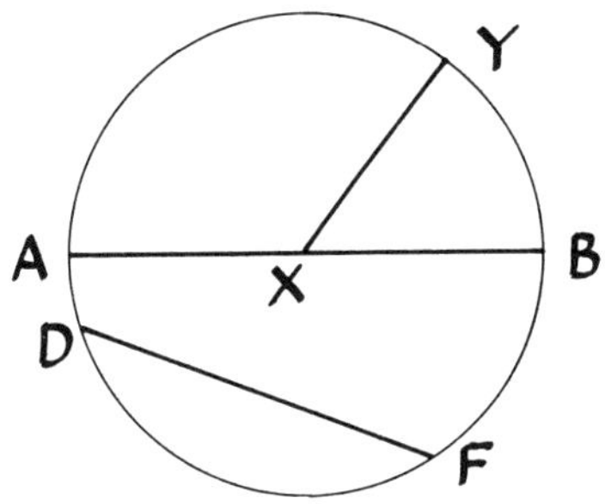

4. Each side of a *cube* is a square, and there are six sides. Each side of a *cube* is ________.
   a. equal to all the other sides
   b. not equal to the other sides
   c. equal to some of the other sides
5. When two lines come together, or *intersect*, they make an angle. Intersect means ________.
   a. make a triangle
   b. come together
   c. never meet

6. In a square opposite sides are parallel. *Parallel* lines never meet. Parallel means ________.
   a. intersect
   b. make an angle
   c. never meet

ROOTS AND PREFIXES

Look at these roots and prefixes from this lesson. You have seen some of them before. Some of them are new.

tri	three
quadr	four
semi	half
dia	through
metr	measure
later	side
therm	heat

Now answer the following questions.

1. How many angles does a triangle have?
2. How many sides do quadrilaterals have?
3. What do you think "lateral" means?
4. What does a thermometer do?
5. Explain the word "diameter."
6. If a magazine is semiannual, how many times does it appear each year? (Hint: annual = yearly.)
7. The clown is riding a unicycle. How many wheels does it have?
8. What is a semicircle?
9. To their surprise, Mr. and Mrs. Gonzalez had quadruplets. How many children did they have at the same time?
10. The United States celebrated its bicentennial in 1976. How old was the country?

11. In South Africa, Black Africans are fighting for equality. What do they want?

PROBLEMS TO SOLVE

Read these problems carefully and find the answers. Many math problems are difficult to understand because of the language. These problems will help you read and understand word problems in math.

1. Look at the map of the three cities: New Castle, Concord, and Smithville.
   a. Is New Castle equidistant from Concord and from Smithville.
   b. Is Concord equidistant from New Castle and Smithville?

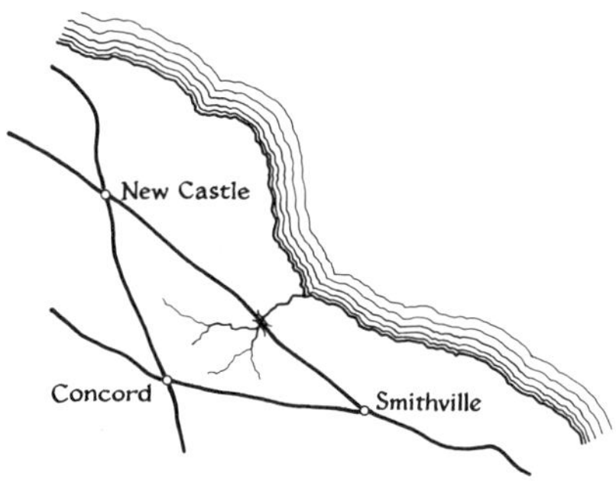

2. The height of a cube is 6 cm. The width is also 6 cm. What is the depth of the cube?
   a. 4 cm b. 5 cm c. 6 cm d. 7 cm
3. If the radius of a circle is 5 cm, what is the diameter?
4. The teacher wanted to be the same distance from each student in the class. The teacher also wanted to see all the students at all times. How did the teacher arrange the chairs in the classroom?
   a. square b. rectangle c. triangle d. semicircle
5. Mary's house is 1 km from Jane's house. Bill's house is 1 km from Mary's house. Jane's house is 1 km from Bill's house. What shape do the three houses make?

ADDITIONAL READING WITH PROBLEMS TO SOLVE

Read the explanation of how to calculate perimeter and area. Then answer the questions and solve the problems that follow.

Perimeters and Areas of Plane Figures

There are important parts to plane geometry. First, it is important to know the area of figures. Area is the space inside the figure. Second, it is important to know the distance around the figures.

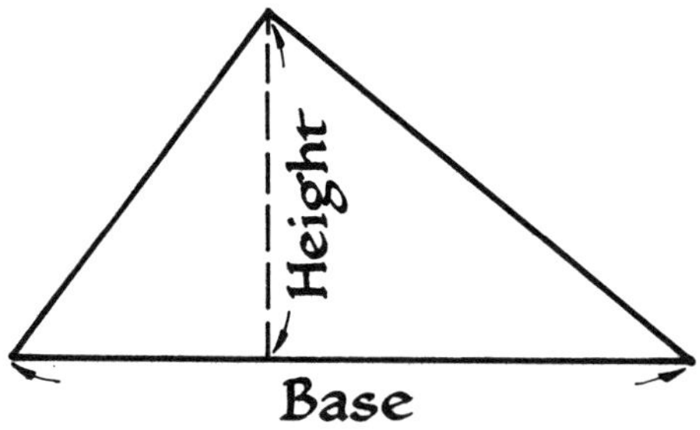

It is easy to find the area of a triangle. Every triangle has a base and a height. To find the area of a triangle, multiply the base by one-half the height ($A = 1/2\ bh$). This will give the area of any triangle. It is not difficult to find the areas of quadrilaterals. For example, the area of a square and a rectangle is the product of two adjacent sides. Adjacent means "next to" or "beside." Multiplying side 1 by side 2 will give the area of each figure. To find the area of a circle, you must use pi (π). Pi equals 3.14 or 22/7. The formula for the area of a circle is pi times the radius squared ($A = \pi r^2$).

The distance around plane figures is easy to find also. For a triangle and for a quadrilateral, add the distances of each side. The distance around a plane figure is a perimeter. There is a different name for the distance around a circle. This is the circumference. To find the circumference, multiply 2 times pi times the radius ($C = 2\ \pi r$).

VOCABULARY IN CONTEXT

Match the word to the definition.

______	1. perimeter	a. distance around a circle
______	2. circumference	b. flat surface
______	3. area	c. space inside a figure
______	4. plane	d. distance around a quadrilateral

PROBLEMS TO SOLVE

1. If the distance from the center of a circle to its outside is 2 cm, what is the distance around the circle.
   a. Will you calculate the circumference or the area?
   b. What formula will you use?
   c. How long is the radius of this circle?

2. A rectangle has two sides of 5 cm and two sides of 3 cm. What is the area? What is its perimeter?
   a. What is the formula for the perimeter of a rectangle?
   b. What is the perimeter?
   c. What is the formula for the area of a rectangle?
   d. What is the area?

3. A pentagon has five equal sides of 2 cm each. What is the perimeter?
   a. What is the easy way to find the perimeter?
   b. What is the perimeter?

4. Mr. and Mrs. Chen want to put new carpeting in their circular living room. The wall is 8 feet from the center of the room. What is the area of the room?
   a. What is the radius?
   b. What formula will you use?
   c. What is the area of the room?

lesson
5

Scientific Notation

preview Mathematicians, scientists, and computer engineers often use scientific notation in their work. Scientific notation makes large and small numbers easy to work with.

$$10^3 = 1000$$

$$10^2 = 100$$

$$10^1 = 10$$

$$10^0 = 1$$

$$10^{-1} = 0.1$$

$$10^{-2} = 0.01$$

$$10^{-3} = 0.001$$

Scientists and mathematicians often use very large numbers with many zeros. For example, one measurement of wavelength is nanometer. It is equal to .000000001 meters. This number has many zeros, so scientists write it like this: 10^{-9}. Scientists use scientific notation to write very, very large or very, very small numbers. It is easy to work with scientific notation because you do not need to write all the zeros.

The system of scientific notation uses numbers with exponents. *Exponents* are little numbers that are above the line. In the number 4^3, the exponent is 3. This figure equals $4 \times 4 \times 4$ or 64. We read 4^3 like this: four to the power of three or four to the third power, or four cubed. In the number 4^2, the exponent is 2. This figure is the same as 4×4 or 16. We read 4^2 like this: four squared.

In scientific notation, exponents show how many digits there are in the number. For example, 10 to the sixth power, or 10 to the sixth, 10^6, is 1,000,000 or 1 million. Ten to the fifth, 10^5, is 100,000 or one hundred thousand. Ten to the fourth, 10^4, is ten thousand or 10,000; ten cubed, 10^3, is one thousand (1,000); 10 squared, 10^2, is one hundred, 100; ten to the first, 10^1, is 10; and 10 to the zero power, 10^0 is 1. Ten to the minus one is .1 or 10^{-1}. Ten to the minus three is 0.001 or 10^{-3}. Ten to the minus seven is .0000001 or 10^{-7}.

If you want to write a number with scientific notation, you must multiply or divide by 10. If you multiply, the decimal point moves to the left, and the exponent is positive. If you divide, the decimal point moves to the right, and the exponent is negative. Study these examples.

$$84{,}562 = 8.4562 \times 10 \times 10 \times 10 \times 10 = 8.4562 \times 10^4$$

← .

$$.005329 = 5.329/10/10/10 = 5.329 \times 10^{-3}$$

→

Scientific notation makes it easy for mathematicians to work with very large or very small numbers because it uses only the important digits, and not the zeros. You will see scientific notation in many areas of science, physics, chemistry, and computers.

354 words ________ time ________ wpm

MAIN IDEA

Choose one main idea for the article about scientific notation. The other ideas may be correct, but one idea is more important than the others.

a. Scientists use scientific notation to write very large and very small numbers.

b. 10^5 shows five places = 10,000.

c. Exponents are small numbers. They are above the line.

d. Scientific notation uses numbers with exponents.

COMPREHENSION QUESTIONS

Write **T** before true statements. Write **F** before false statements. Use the information from the article, but do not look at the article.

_______ 1. Scientists use scientific notation to write very large numbers.

_______ 2. With scientific notation, you need to write all the zeros.

_______ 3. Scientific notation uses numbers with exponents.

_______ 4. In the number 4^3, the exponent is 4.

_______ 5. Five cubed = 5^3.

_______ 6. Four times four is four squared.

_______ 7. Scientific notation uses exponents to show the power of 10.

_______ 8. Ten to the fourth power is one thousand.

_______ 9. Exponents can be negative or positive.

_______ 10. *Scientific notation is important in many sciences.

_______ number answered correctly

Write the line number of the sentence that states the main idea of this article. _________

Write the line number of the sentence or sentences that support your answer to question 10. _________

USING NEW VOCABULARY

Do this exercise if your score on the comprehension questions was under 7 or if you want more practice with the new words. Did you understand the new words? Read the article again and answer these questions. Look at the new words, but *do not* use your dictionary.

1. How big is a nanometer?
2. How do scientists write .000000001?
3. What kinds of numbers do scientists write with scientific notation?
4. Why do scientists use scientific notation?
5. What are exponents?
6. Write these numbers with exponents.
   4 squared
   5 cubed
   3 to the tenth power
   5 to the minus three
7. What do exponents show?
8. Write these as whole numbers.
   10^6
   10^{-4}
   10^4
   10^{-6}
9. Which way does the decimal point move if the exponent is positive?
10. If the exponent is negative, which way does the decimal point move?
11. Who uses scientific notation?

ROOTS AND PREFIXES REVIEW

These words come from Latin or Greek roots. Use the prefixes and roots that you have studied. Try to guess the meaning of the italicized word. Circle the meaning.

1. The students *united* to cook the dinner and put on a show for the faculty.
   a. made one group
   b. divided into two groups
   c. didn't work together
2. Michael's wife had *triplets* last week.
   a. one baby
   b. two babies
   c. three babies

3. The university celebrated its *centennial* last year. How old was the university?
   a. 10 years
   b. 100 years
   c. 1,000 years
4. The school children usually wear *uniforms.*
   a. They wear the same clothes.
   b. They wear only one dress.
   c. They wear different clothes.
5. The Civil Rights Act gave *equality* to Black Americans.
   a. It said they were different from other Americans.
   b. It said they were the same color as other Americans.
   c. It gave them the same rights as other Americans.
6. The children *averted* their eyes when the teacher was angry with them.
   a. They looked at the teacher.
   b. They turned their eyes away from the teacher.
   c. The teacher looked at the children.
7. To *convert* kilos to pounds, multiply by 2.2.
   a. change
   b. measure
   c. return

ADDITIONAL READING WITH PROBLEMS TO SOLVE

Read about adding, subtracting, multiplying, and dividing with scientific notation and then solve the following problems.

Basic Operations with Scientific Notation

It is not difficult to add, subtract, multiply, or divide numbers with scientific notation. Before you can add or subtract two numbers, the exponents must be the same. For example, add 1.63×10^4 and 2.8×10^3. First, convert the exponents. Make them the same value. Change 2.8×10^3 to $.28 \times 10^4$. Now you can add.

$$\begin{array}{r} 1.63 \times 10^4 \\ + \underline{.28 \times 10^4} \\ 1.91 \times 10^4 \end{array}$$

If you want to multiply or divide numbers with exponents, you do not need to change the exponents. To multiply, add the powers of 10. For example, 6×10^6 multiplied by 2×10^{-4} equals 12×10^2. To divide numbers with exponents, subtract the exponents. For example, 6×10^6 divided by 2×10^{-4} equals 3×10^{10}.

Problems

1. Convert the following measurements to scientific notation.
   a. 1,380 km
   b. 980.7 cm
   c. 865,000 mi
   d. .00009004 g
2. Write the following numbers in ordinary decimal notation.
   a. 4.5023×10^5
   b. 6.8×10^{-3}
   c. 796×10^3
   d. 4.186×10^7
3. Subtract 9.26×10^{-4} kg from 4.575×10^{-2} kg.
4. Multiply 2.4×10^6 by 6.25×10^{-4}
5. Compute $\dfrac{(1.56 \times 10^2) \times (2.0 \times 10^{-4})}{5.2 \times 10^5}$
6. Calculate $\dfrac{1}{(4.0 \times 10^{11}) \times (5.25 \times 10^{-5})}$
7. One light-minute is the distance light travels in one minute. Calculate the approximate number of miles in one light-minute. Use scientific notation for calculations.

   speed of light = 186,000 mi/s   1 min = 60 s
8. Evaluate $\dfrac{(9.0 \times 10^9) \times (1.6 \times 10^{-19})2}{(2 \times 10^{-15})}$ to two significant figures.

chapter 2

Science

lesson 6

Scientific Classification

preview Preview this lesson by discussing the diagram with your teacher and classmates. Look at the pictures in the margin, and read the first paragraph. What do you think the main idea of this article is going to be?

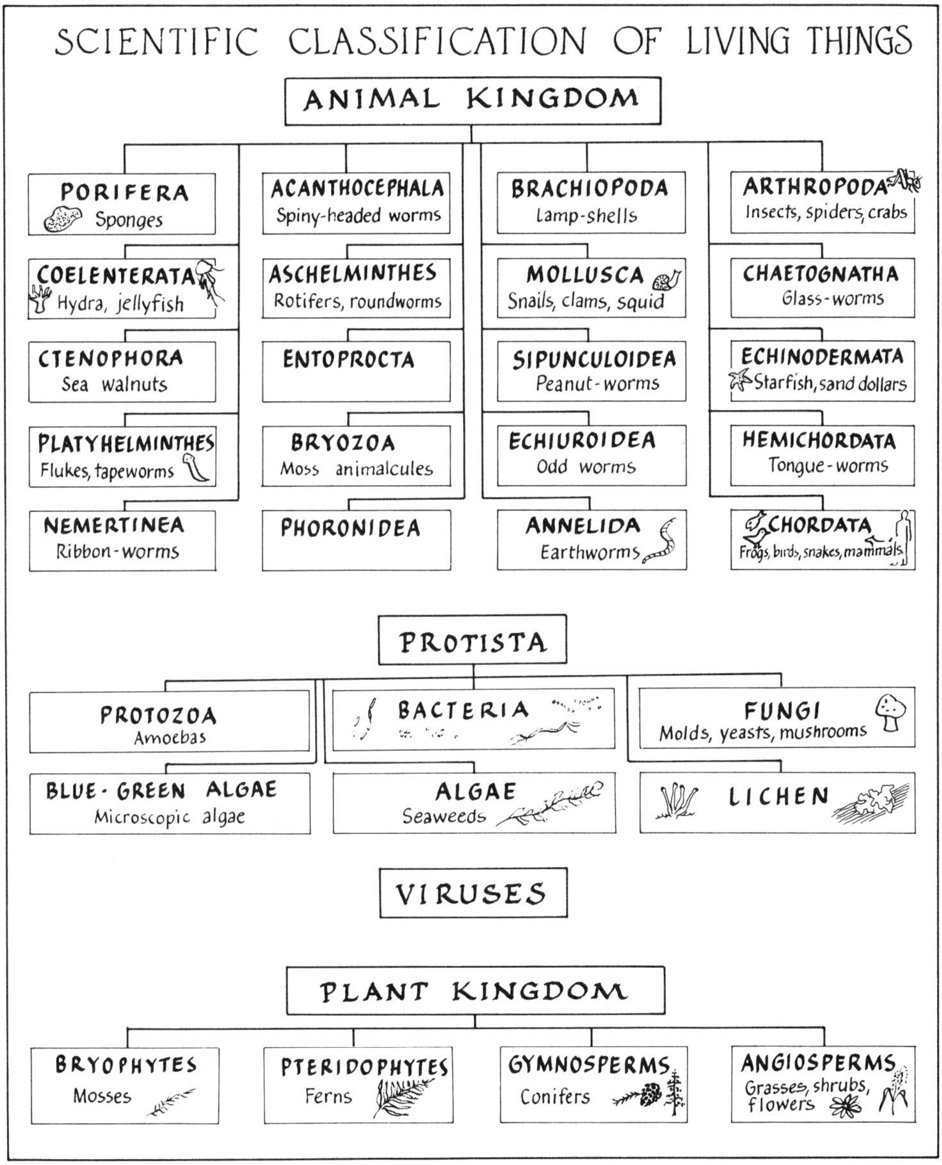

The Swedish botanist Carolus Linnaeus began the modern scientific classification system. He divided plants and animals by their structures or parts, and he gave each species a different two-part name. His system is easy for botanists, biologists, and zoologists from all over the world to use in talking about the same plants and animals.

Linnaeus's system of scientific classification is important for two reasons. He was the first botanist to classify plants into groups by their parts. He looked at the different parts of the plants and put plants with the same parts into the same group. Second, he gave each plant two names: one name for genus and one name for species. For example, the sunflower is a large yellow flower common in North and South America. The scientific name for it is *Helianthus annuus*. *Helianthus* is the genus name, and *annuus* is the species. The robin is a red bird. Its scientific name is *Turdus migratorius*. *Turdus* is the genus name, and *migratorius* is the species name.

Many scientific names are Latin or Greek because the scientists in the eighteenth and nineteenth centuries used these languages to study and teach. Look at the scientific name of the robin. *Turdus* means "thrush" in Latin. A thrush is a kind of bird. *Migratorius* comes from Latin and means "to move from place to place." A robin is a thrush or bird that moves from place to place. Each year, the robins fly south in the fall; they return north in the spring. In parts of the United States, the robin is the first sign of spring.

The name of the scientific classification system also comes from Latin. This two-name classification is called binomial nomenclature. *Binomial* means "two name," and *nomenclature* means "system of naming." Binomial nomenclature gives each plant or animal two scientific names. Then it is easy for scientists from different countries to talk about the same living thing. Each plant or animal has only one scientific name, but it may have a different common name in each area. For example, *Canis latrans* is the scientific name for a wolflike animal. It has different names in different parts of the United States. It is known as the prairie wolf, the bush wolf, the little wolf, and the coyote.

Carolus Linnaeus was a Swedish botanist. He lived in the eighteenth century from the years 1707 to 1778. Linnaeus studied plants and began to use a system for scientific classification. He divided all living things into two kingdoms: the plant kingdom and the animal kingdom. Today biologists, botanists, and zoologists from all over the world use his system of classification, although they have made some changes.

447 words ________ time ________ wpm

MAIN IDEA

Choose one main idea for this article. All the statements may be true, but one is the main idea of the article.

a. The scientific name for robin is *Turdus migratorius*.

b. C. Linnaeus liked to study plants.

c. C. Linnaeus established a two-name classification system.

d. Many scientific names come from Latin or Greek.

Choose three reasons why Linnaeus's binomial classification is important.

a. It classifies plants and animals with similar parts in the same groups.

b. It uses Latin and Greek names.

c. It classifies each animal or plant with two scientific names.

d. It is 250 years old.

e. It is easy for scientists all over the world to use.

COMPREHENSION QUESTIONS

Write **T** before true statements. Write **F** before false statements. *Do not* look back at the reading, and *do not* use your dictionary.

_______ 1. Linnaeus divided plants by their different colors.

_______ 2. Linnaeus classified living things into two main groups: animals and plants.

_______ 3. He gave every plant two names.

_______ 4. Scientists don't use the Linnaeus classification system now.

_______ 5. Linnaeus studied only birds.

_______ 6. "Robin" is a common name, and *Turdus migratorius* is a scientific name.

_______ 7. Many scientific names are either Latin or Greek.

_______ 8. Binomial nomenclature gives each living thing a genus and a species name.

_____ 9. Linneaus's classification system is the binomial system.

_____ 10. *Botanists study animals.

_____ 11. *Botanists in the the seventeenth century did not understand Greek or Latin.

_____ 12. The coyote has only one common name.

_____ number answered correctly

Write the line number of the sentence that states the main idea of this article. _____

Write the line number of the sentence or sentences that support your answer to questions 10 _____ and 11 _____.

USING NEW VOCABULARY

Do this exercise if your score on the comprehension questions was under 9 or if you want more practice with the new vocabulary. Did you understand the new words and ideas? Read the article again and answer these questions. *Do not* use your dictionary.

1. What country did Linnaeus come from?
2. Did he live in the seventeenth century?
3. How old was he when he died?
4. What did he study?
5. How did he divide all living things?
6. Who uses his system of classification now?
7. How did Linnaeus classify plants?
8. How many names did Linnaeus give each plant?
9. Where do many scientific names come from?
10. What language did scientists and teachers use in the 1700s?
11. What does *turdus* mean?
12. What does *migratorius* mean?

13. What is a robin?
14. Where do robins go in winter?
15. Why is Linnaeus's system called *binomial nomenclature*?
16. How many common names does the coyote have?
17. Why is it easy for scientists from different parts of the world to talk about the same animal?

ROOTS

Many scientific names come from Latin and Greek. If you study science, you will learn many roots. Study them and they will help you learn other English words too. Look at these words from the lesson and their meanings.

botanist	a scientist who studies plants
botany	the study of plants
zoologist	a scientist who studies animals
zoology	the study of animals
biologist	a scientist who studies living things
biology	the study of living things
binomial	with two names (bi- = two)
nomenclature	system of naming
migrate	move from place to place

Learn these roots and suffixes. A *suffix* goes at the end of a word.

bot	plant
migr	move
nom	name
zoo	animal
bio	life
-ology	the study of
-ist	the person who

Read these sentences and answer the questions that follow.

1. Biology is a science.

   What do biologists study? ________
2. The students are reading a biography of Martin Luther King.

   What are they reading about? ________
3. The children like to visit the zoo.

   What do they see there? ________
4. Some birds migrate to warmer places in the winter.

   Do they stay in the same place all year? ________
5. Zootheism is a kind of religion.

   What kind of gods do the people have? ________
6. Many of the fruits and vegetables in the United States are picked by

   migrant workers. Do these workers live in one place all year? ________
7. If "anthro" means human beings, what is anthropology? ________
8. What is an anthropologist? ________

QUESTIONS FOR DISCUSSION

1. Can you think of other ways to classify plants and animals?
2. Discuss different ways of classifying
   a. the students in your class
   b. the businesses in your city
   c. sports

lesson 7

Green Plants

preview Discuss the illustration and the importance of green plants with your teacher and classmates.

Plants are necessary for life on earth. All living things need plants because they provide food for animals. During photosynthesis, plants change the sun's energy into food and energy for animals. They use carbon dioxide (CO_2) and produce oxygen. All human beings and animals need oxygen to live.

During photosynthesis, all the parts of a plant work together to produce food. Plants have three important parts: roots, stems, and leaves. Two other parts are flowers and fruit.

Roots usually grow underground. They help keep the plant in the soil. They also absorb water and minerals from the soil and then carry them to the other parts of the plant. In some plants, such as carrots or potatoes, the roots store food for the plants.

Plant *stems* are usually above the ground. They hold the leaves and flowers. There are two kinds of stems. The stems of many flowers and vegetables are soft and green. They bend easily. These plants live for only one year. They are *annual* plants. Other plants have hard and woody stems. Trees have brown, woody stems. They are *perennial* plants. They live for several years.

Leaves are an important part of the plant. The leaves grow on the stem. Most leaves are green because they contain chlorophyll. Chlorophyll is necessary for photosynthesis. The leaves make food for the plant. This food gives energy for the other parts of the plant.

In the process of photosynthesis, roots, stems, and leaves of green plants work together to make sugar from sunlight. *Photosynthesis* is a Greek word. It means "putting together with light." During the process of photosynthesis, plants use sunlight, chlorophyll, carbon dioxide (CO_2), and water to make food. In this way, green plants use the sun's energy to make food for the plant and other living things. Other living organisms, such as animals, get their energy by eating the plants. Human beings eat both animals and plants to get energy. Without green plants, the sun's energy could not be used on the earth, and all other organisms living on the earth would die.

345 words ________ time ________ wpm

MAIN IDEA

Choose the main idea of this article.

a. Plants have only three parts.
b. Plants are necessary for life.
c. Annual plants have green stems.
d. Leaves are an important part of the plant.

COMPREHENSION QUESTIONS

Write **T** before true statements. Write **F** before false statements. *Do not* look at the article.

______ 1. Plants are necessary for life.

______ 2. Plants supply food for animals.

______ 3. Roots, stems, and leaves are not parts of plants.

______ 4. Flowers and fruits are parts of plants.

______ 5. Roots are often above ground.

______ 6. Roots sometimes store food for the plants.

______ 7. Roots, stems, and leaves are the only parts of plants.

______ 8. The stems of all plants are soft and green.

______ 9. The plant makes sugar by a process of photosynthesis.

______ 10. Leaves contain chlorophyll.

______ 11. Leaves make food for the plant.

______ 12. *Sunlight, carbon dioxide, chlorophyll, and water are necessary for photosynthesis.

______ number answered correctly

Write the line number of the sentence that states the main idea of this article. ________

Write the line number of the sentence or sentences that support your answer to question 12.

USING NEW VOCABULARY

Do this exercise if your score on the comprehension questions was less than 8 or if you want to practice the new words. Did you understand the new words and ideas? Read the article again and answer these questions. *Do not* use your dictionary.

1. What do plants give animals.?
2. What do plants make from the sun's energy?
3. What do human beings and animals need to live?
4. What are five parts of plants?
5. Where do roots grow?
6. What do the roots take from the soil?
7. What do the roots of carrots and potatoes do?
8. Where are plant stems?
9. What do the stems hold?
10. What kind of stems do flowers have?
11. How long do annual plants live?
12. What kind of stems do trees have?
13. How long do perennial plants live?
14. Where do the leaves of plants grow?
15. Why are leaves green?
16. What do the leaves do?
17. What do plants make from sunlight?
18. What is the name of this process?
19. Why are green plants important for human beings?
20. If necessary, reread the article. Look for these words: root, stem, and leaf. Write the words on the lines in the diagram.

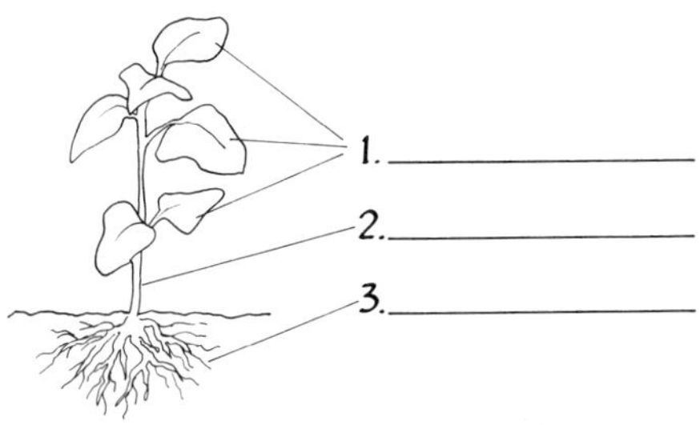

VOCABULARY IN CONTEXT

Reread the article. Find these words. The line number is in parentheses. Match the meaning with the word. *Do not* use your dictionary; try to guess the meaning from the context.

______	1. provide (2)	a. live for only one year
______	2. absorb (10)	b. supply; make
______	3. store (12)	c. live for many years
______	4. annual plants (16)	d. process to make food in plants
______	5. perennial plants (17)	e. keep; hold until later
______	6. photosynthesis (21)	f. take in water

ADDITIONAL READING

Read this article about cells. Write the names of the cell parts on the picture.

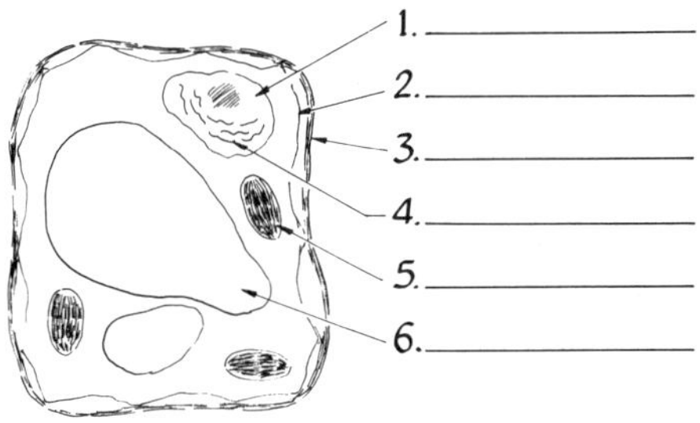

Cells

Cells are the smallest part (unit) of life. All living things are made of cells, and all cells have the same parts: nucleus, cytoplasm, and membrane. The *nucleus* is the center of the cell. It contains the chromosomes and the genes. The *genes* carry the information that tells the cell what to do. Chromosomes and genes help to make new cells. The *cytoplasm* surrounds the nucleus in the cell. It contains several different things. Different kinds of cells have different things in their cytoplasm. The *cell membrane* is around the cell. The membrane controls the flow of liquids in and out of the cell.

Plant cells are different from animal cells. In addition to the nucleus, cytoplasm, and membrane, they contain a cell wall, vacuoles, and chloroplasts. The *cell wall* is around the membrane. It is made of cellulose, and it is not living. It gives plant cells a shape like a box. *Vacuoles* are round structures in the cytoplasm. A membrane surrounds them, and they contain water and other things. The cell uses the vacuoles to store things. They sometimes contain pigments. These pigments give flower cells their colors. *Chloroplasts* are also in the cytoplasm. They contain a green pigment, chlorophyl, and they make food for the plant. Chloroplasts are necessary for photosynthesis.

Life Science, Jenne Taylor Richardson, Anne F. Harris, Oliver Crosby Sparks, Silver Burdett Company, Morristown, New Jersey, 1979.

lesson
8

Microscopic Organisms

preview Discuss the title and illustration with your teacher and classmates. Read the first paragraph, and write down what you think the main idea will be.

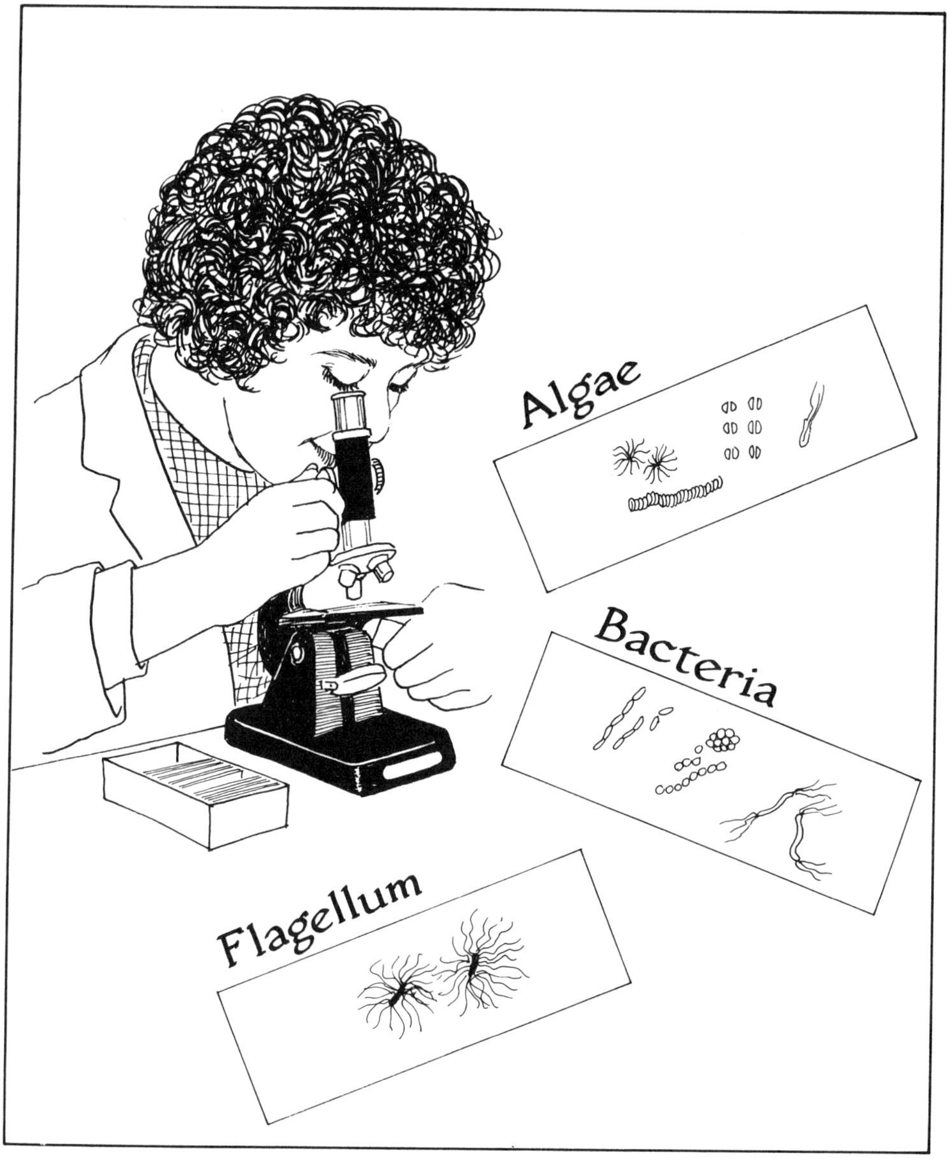

In the seventeenth century, Antonie van Leeuwenhoek was the first person to see tiny organisms with a microscope. He called them *animalcules*. Later, scientists in the eighteenth and nineteenth centuries named these animalcules bacteria and protozoa. This was the beginning of the sciences of bacteriology and protozoology, the studies of microscopic organisms. Bacteriologists and protozoologists have studied these organisms for many years, but it is difficult to classify them.

Scientists cannot classify some of these microscopic organisms in the plant or animal kingdom, so they put them into another kingdom, protist. Some protists are like animals. They do not have chlorophyll, and they cannot make their own food. These protists get their food from other organisms.

Other protists are like plants. They have chlorophyll, and they can make their own food. They usually live in water. Both animal and plantlike protists provide food for other plants and animals that live in the water. Many protists are single-celled organisms. They have only one cell. Others, however, are multicelled. They have many cells. Because these organisms are neither plants nor animals, scientists put them in another kingdom.

Bacteria are also difficult to classify in the plant or animal kingdoms. They have only one cell, but the cell does not have a nucleus. It contains only a cell membrane and a cell wall. Bacteria cannot make their own food. They must get the food from other organisms. Some bacteriologists classify bacteria separately in the monera kingdom.

Another microscopic organism is the virus. It is much smaller than protists or bacteria. Scientists can see it only with the electron microscope. A virus is not a cell. It is simpler than a cell. It does not have a cytoplasm or a nucleus. It has a cover of protein, and inside the protein, there is reproductive material. This reproductive material helps the virus reproduce. It makes more viruses.

The virus reproduces only when it is inside another cell. When it enters another cell, it begins to reproduce. It makes more and more viruses inside the cell until the cell breaks open and the viruses go into other cells. For this reason, scientists have difficulty classifying it as living or nonliving. Outside another cell, the virus is inactive. It does not become active and reproduce until it enters another cell.

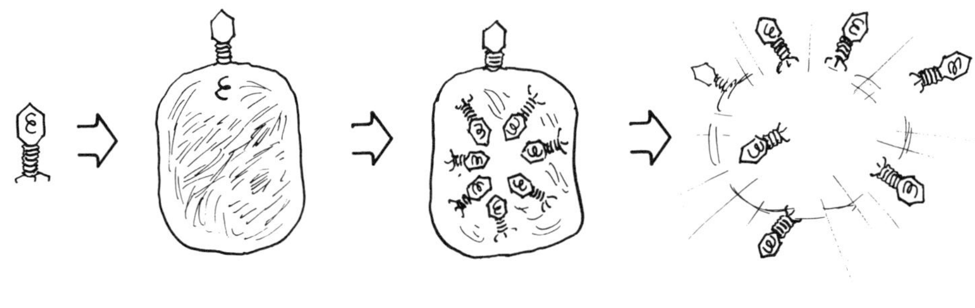

Although we cannot see them, microscopic organisms are everywhere. They are an important part of life on the earth. It is difficult to classify these organisms, because they are different from other plants and animals. Some of them have chlorophyll like plants, and others do not. Some of them are not complete cells. Bacteria do not have a nucleus, and viruses do not have cytoplasm. To help classify microscopic organisms, some bacteriologists have added two more kingdoms: the protists and the monera.

466 words ________ time ________ wpm

MAIN IDEA

Choose the main idea of this article.

a. It is difficult to classify microscopic organisms.
b. Microscopic organisms are very small.
c. Viruses cause many dangerous diseases which doctors cannot cure.
d. Some protists are like animals and some are like plants.

Circle three reasons why microscopic organisms are difficult to classify.

a. Some are not like either plants or animals.
b. Some are plants because they have chlorophyll.
c. Some are not complete cells.
d. Some are animals and cannot make their own food by photosynthesis.
e. Some have different shapes.
f. Scientists are not sure if some are living or nonliving.

COMPREHENSION QUESTIONS

Write **T** before true statements. Write **F** before false statements. *Do not* look at the article.

______ 1. Bacteriologists study microscopic organisms.

______ 2. All microscopic organisms have only one cell.

______ 3. Microscopic organisms belong to the animal kingdom.

______ 4. *It is easy to classify microscopic organisms.

______ 5. Animal-like protists can make their own food from chlorophyll.

______ 6. Plantlike protists have chlorophyll.

______ 7. A virus is a cell.

______ 8. Animalcules are bacteria and protozoa.

______ 9. The protist and monera kingdoms include microscopic organisms.

______ 10. A virus becomes active inside another cell.

______ 11. *All microscopic organisms are part of the plant kingdom.

______ 12. *We need a microscope to see bacteria and other microscopic organisms.

______ number answered correctly

After correcting your answers, go back to the article to find out the reason for the correct answer. Try to understand new words from the context.

Write the line number of the sentence that states the main idea of this article. ________

Write the line number of the sentence or sentences that support your answer to questions 4, ________ 11 ________, and 12 ________.

VOCABULARY IN CONTEXT

Reread the article. Find the following words. The line number is in parentheses. Write a short definition of each word.

1. bacteriology (5) ______________________
2. protozoology (5) ______________________
3. single-celled (16) ______________________
4. multicelled (17) ______________________
5. reproduce (30) ______________________

6. living cells (34) ____________________

7. nonliving cells (35) ____________________

ROOTS AND PREFIXES

Read these sentences; then guess the meaning of the root.

1. A microscope is an instrument for seeing tiny organisms.
   A telescope is an instrument for seeing things far away.

   scope means ____________________.

2. A multicelled organism has many cells.
   A multinational company works in many countries.

   multi means ____________________.

3. Annual plants live for one year.

   annu means ____________________.

4. Photosynthesis is a process using light.
   Photography is a process of making pictures from light.

   photo means ____________________.

5. A microscope is an instrument for seeing very small organisms.
   A microorganism is a very small, tiny organism.

   micro means ____________________.

6. Reproduce means to produce again or to make more.
   Repeat means to say something again.

   re means ____________________.

Read these sentences. Use your knowledge of roots to guess the meaning of the italicized word. Answer the questions that follow.

1. His father is a millionaire, but his grandfather is a *multimillionaire*. Who is richer?

2. In the summertime the crickets *multiply*. Do we have more or fewer crickets in the summertime?

3. Next month is my parents' twenty-fifth *anniversary*. How many years have they been married?

4. That magazine is published *annually*. How often is it published?

5. *Microcomputers* are very popular these days. Why?
6. How are *microwaves* different from radio waves?
7. Astronomers study the stars in the sky. Why do they use a *telescope*?
8. Where does a *photoelectric* cell get its energy?

Study and learn these new roots and prefixes.

micro	small
scope	to look, see
annu	year
photo	light
re	again

ADDITIONAL READING

Read this paragraph about bacteria. Then fill in the outline below. List two ways bacteria are harmful and five ways they are useful.

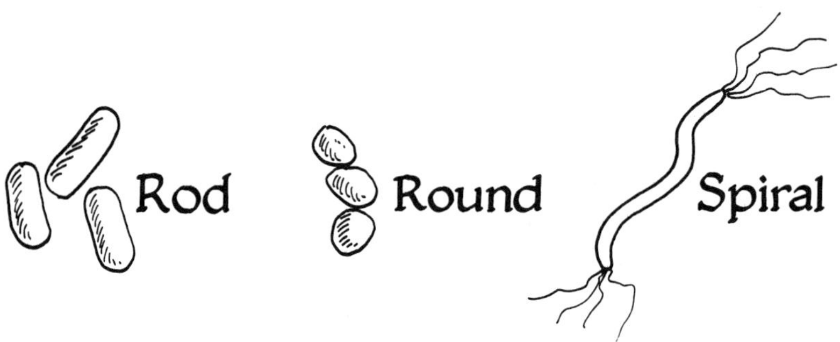

Bacteria

Bacteria live everywhere: in the air, in the soil, and in the water. They live in and on the bodies of plants and animals. There are more bacteria than any other kind of organism in the world. There are three kinds of bacteria. They have different shapes. They are spiral (*spirillus*), round (*coccus*), and rod shaped (*bacillus*). Some bacteria are harmful. They are not good for human beings. They make food spoil so that we cannot eat it. They also cause many dangerous diseases, such as scarlet fever, tuberculosis, and cholera.

Most bacteria, however, are useful. They help human beings. They produce necessary chemicals. Bacteria help dead plants and animals decay. They make nitrogen for plants. They help make some foods such as vinegar and cheese. Some bacteria, like penicillin, produce antibodies, and these antibodies fight and prevent disease. Bacteria, both useful and harmful, are everywhere.

Life Science, Jenne Taylor Richardson, Anne F. Harris, Oliver Crosby Sparks, Silver Burdett Company, Morristown, New Jersey, 1979 (juvenile).

Bacteria are harmful because

a. ______________________________

b. ______________________________

Bacteria are useful because

a. ______________________________

b. ______________________________

c. ______________________________

d. ______________________________

e. ______________________________

Questions for Discussion

1. What is the difference between bacteria and viruses?
2. AIDS, Legionnaire's Disease, and influenza are viral diseases. How do doctors treat these and other viral diseases?

lesson
9

Energy

preview Look at the illustrations and pictures in this article about energy. What is energy? Read the article to find out what forms it takes.

The word *energy* has different uses. In the sentence "Young people have more energy than old people," it means strength, power, and activity. In physics, energy is a very important idea. It is the ability to do work, and it has two forms.

In physics there are two forms of energy: kinetic and potential. *Kinetic* energy is movement or motion. A moving car has kinetic energy. If it hits another car, it will damage the other car. The amount of kinetic energy depends on the size and speed of the car. A truck can do more damage than a bicycle, and a car going 50 mph can do more damage than a car going 5 mph.

The formula $KE = 1/2\ mv^2$ represents kinetic energy. In other words, kinetic energy is one-half of the object's mass (size) multiplied by its velocity (speed) squared.

Potential energy is the energy inside something. Wood has potential energy. Oxygen (O) has potential energy. Burning the wood releases, or lets out, the energy. Processes that release energy are *exothermic* processes. Processes that absorb energy are *endothermic* processes. The total energy of an object is the sum of its potential and kinetic energy.

The amount of total energy in the universe is constant. The amount of energy does not change. There is no new energy. No energy is lost. This is the *law of conservation of energy*. There is never more energy, and there is never less energy.

Energy does change, however. It can change from one form to another. This process is *transformation of energy*. Energy may change from water to electricity. Light, sound, electricity, and heat are ways to transmit energy.

Most of the world's energy comes from the sun. Plants produce food for energy during photosynthesis. The sun's energy is in wood, oil, and other things that people use for energy.

People use many sources of energy. Ancient people used only their arms, hands, and simple tools until they discovered fire. Later, people learned to use the energy of the wind to sail ships. Then they learned to use animals to do work. In the eighteenth and nineteenth centuries, people began to use machines. The first machines used steam. They burned coal to heat water. The hot water turned into steam, and the steam engine did the work. Later, people began to use the gasoline engine, and today people are using nuclear energy. There are many sources of energy.

Energy is one of the basic concepts, or ideas, of physics. It is the ability to do work. There are two forms of energy and two important laws that explain energy. Without energy we could not live. We need energy to work, and scientists are always looking for new sources of energy.

461 words ________ time ________ wpm

MAIN IDEA

Choose the main idea of this article.

a. There are two kinds of energy.
b. There are many sources of energy.
c. Energy is the ability to do work, and it is a basic concept in physics.
d. The law of conservation of energy means that the amount of energy does not change.

COMPREHENSION QUESTIONS

Mark the statements **T** if they are true or **F** if they are false. *Do not* look back at the article.

_______ 1. The word *energy* has only one meaning.

_______ 2. Energy is the ability to do work.

_______ 3. There are two kinds of energy.

_______ 4. A moving car has potential energy.

_______ 5. The amount of kinetic energy depends on the size and speed of the object.

_______ 6. At the same speed, a small car has more kinetic energy than a large truck.

_______ 7. Objects cannot have both kinetic and potential energy.

_______ 8. *Potential energy is either exothermic or endothermic.

_______ 9. When we use energy, we finish the supply. The energy is lost.

_______ 10. None of the world's energy comes from the sun.

_______ 11. Wind, steam, and gasoline are sources of energy.

_______ 12. *We need new sources of energy.

_______ number answered correctly

After correcting your answers, go back to the article and find out the reason for the correct answer. Try to understand the words from the context.

Write the line number of the sentence that states the main idea of this article. ________

Write the line number of the sentence or sentences that support your answer to questions 8 ________ and 12 ________.

OUTLINE

This article about energy has four parts. Answer the questions and complete the outline.

I. What are two definitions of energy?

A. ______________________________

B. ______________________________

II. What are two kinds of energy?

A. ______________________________

B. ______________________________

III. What are two laws of energy?

A. ______________________________

B. ______________________________

IV. What are eight sources of energy?

1. ______________________________
2. ______________________________
3. ______________________________
4. ______________________________
5. ______________________________
6. ______________________________
7. ______________________________
8. ______________________________

VOCABULARY IN CONTEXT

Find these words in the text. The line numbers are in parentheses. Write a brief definition from the text.

1. kinetic energy (6) ______________________
2. potential energy (14) ______________________
3. endothermic (17) ______________________
4. exothermic (16) ______________________
5. law of conservation of energy (21) ______________________
6. transformation of energy (24) ______________________

ROOTS AND PREFIXES

Read these sentences and guess the meaning of the root.

1. Transmit means to send something from one place to another.
   Transport means to carry something from one place to another.

   trans = ________.

2. A thermometer measures heat.
   A thermal blanket heats your bed.

   therm = ________.

3. Exothermic means that the heat or energy goes out.
   Exit is the way out of a room or building.

   ex and exo = ________.

4. Transmit means to send across a distance.
   Submit means to send in.

   mit(t), miss = ________.

5. Invert means to turn over.
   Revert means to turn back.

   vert = ________.

Read the sentences and answer the questions.

1. To conserve energy, keep your thermostat set at 68° F.

   The thermostat controls the ________ in the house.

2. My brother carries soup in a thermos bottle in his lunch box.

   The thermos keeps the soup ________.

3. The dentist extracted my bad tooth. What does *extract* mean?

4. When we breathe we inhale oxygen (O) and exhale carbon dioxide (CO_2). What does *exhale* mean?
5. My plane stopped in Amsterdam, and I waited in the transit lounge. Did I plan to stay in the Netherlands or continue my trip.
6. It was a trans-Atlantic flight. Was the flight from New York to Amsterdam, or from Bahrain to Amsterdam?
7. To find the reciprocal of a fraction, invert the fraction. How do you find the reciprocal?

Study and learn these roots.

trans	across
therm	heat
ex, exo	out of
mit(t), miss	send
vert	turn

ADDITIONAL READING

Read this paragraph about heat measurement. Then solve the problems that follow.

Measurement of Heat

All forms of energy end as *heat*. Heat is energy. A way to measure heat is to take the *temperature*. Temperature is a measurement of heat. A *thermometer* is an instrument to measure temperature.

There are three scales that measure temperature: Fahrenheit, Celsius, and Kelvin. The freezing and boiling points are different on these scales.

	F°	C°	K	
boiling	212	100	317.15	water boils
freezing	32	0	273.15	ice melts
	−459.69	−273.15	absolute 0	

We use the Fahrenheit and Celsius scales every day to measure heat. Scientists use the Kelvin scale. The units in the Kelvin and the

Centigrade scales are the same size, but the boiling and freezing points are different. Units on the Fahrenheit and Celsius scales are degrees, so we read a temperature of 37°C like this: thirty-seven degrees Centigrade. The units of the Kelvin scale are kelvins, so we read a Kelvin temperature like this: two hundred and seventy-five kelvins. Here are some formulas to convert temperatures from one scale to the other.

$$C = F - 32 \times 5/9$$

$$F = C \times 5/9 + 32$$

$$K = C + 273$$

$$C = K - 273$$

Problems to Solve

1. Normal body temperature is 98.6°F. What is this in degrees Celsius?
2. Gallium metal melts at 30°C and boils at 1,983°C. What are its melting and boiling points in kelvins?
3. Electric light bulbs use the element tungsten. Its boiling point is 5,927°C. What is its boiling point expressed in kelvins?
4. Dry ice (CO_2) has a temperature of 195° K. What is its temperature on the Celsius scale?
5. A certain brand of cigarettes gives off 7.0 mg of tar per cigarette. If a smoker consumes two packs of cigarettes per day (at twenty cigarettes per pack), how many kilograms of tar would be given off by the cigarettes in one year of 365 days?

Problems 2, 3, 4, and 5 adapted from *General Chemistry*, 2d edition, SI version, by James E. Brady and Gerald E. Humiston (New York: John Wiley and Sons, 1980), pp. 26–27.

Questions for Discussion

1. How does potential energy differ from kinetic energy?
2. What is meant by endothermic and exothermic?
3. What is the difference between heat and temperature?

lesson 10

Atoms

preview Atomic and nuclear energy are becoming important sources of energy. Nuclear energy comes from dividing the atom. Read this article to learn about the basic parts of the atom. Before you begin to read, look at the illustrations.

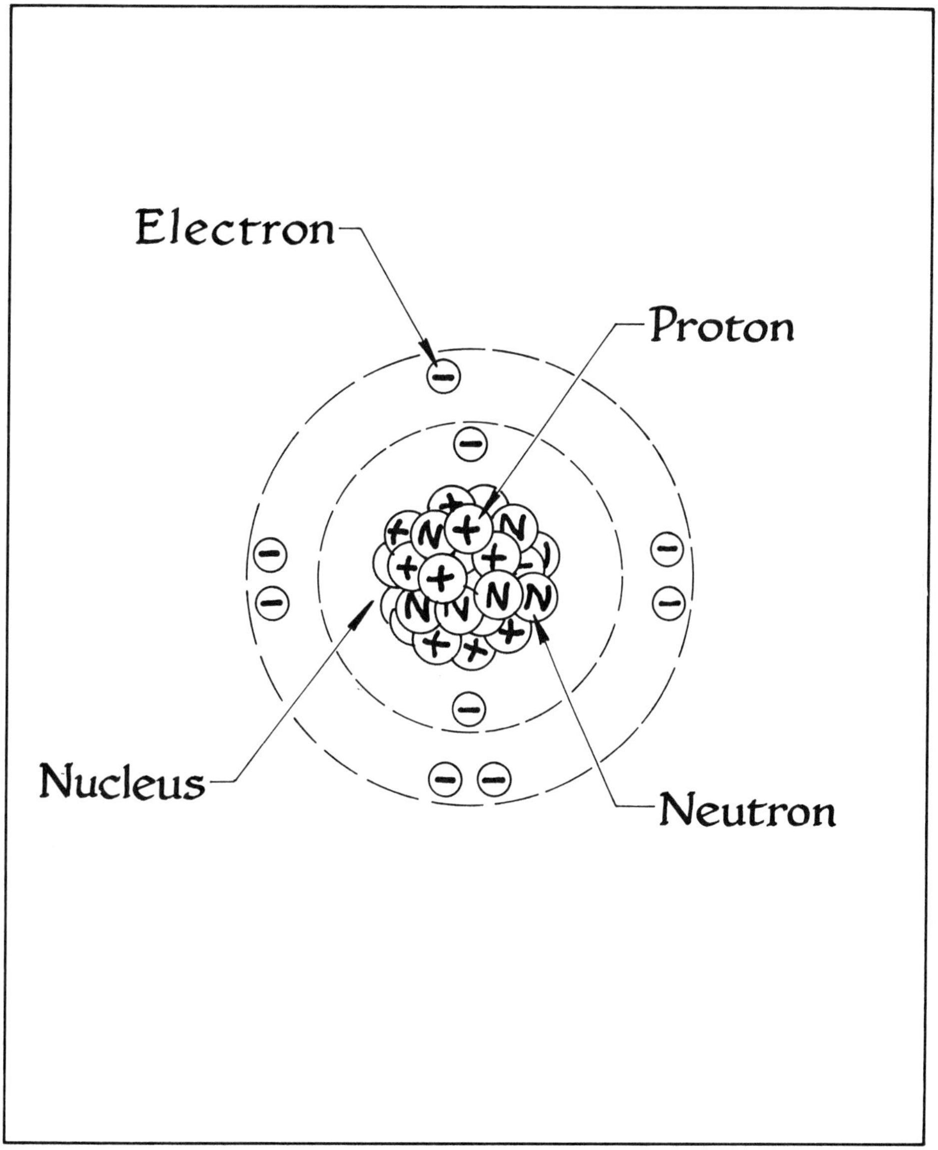

Energy and matter are the two basic ideas in physics. Anything that takes up space and has weight is *matter*. It can be solid, liquid, or gas. For example, ice is solid, water is liquid, and vapor is gas. Matter must have both volume and weight. Light and heat do not have weight, so they are not matter; they are energy. Matter is everywhere around us. Scientists study matter and divide it into smaller and smaller parts.

The smaller parts that scientists divide matter into are called molecules. A *molecule* is the smallest part of something that is itself. For example, a molecule of water (H_2O) is two parts hydrogen and one part oxygen. A molecule is the smallest part of water. Hydrogen and oxygen alone are not water.

Scientists divide molecules into smaller parts. These smaller parts are *atoms*. A sugar molecule contains three different kinds of atoms. One molecule of sugar has twelve carbon (C) atoms, twenty-two hydrogen (H) atoms, and eleven oxygen (O) atoms. Atoms are small pieces of matter. At present, scientists know about 100 different kinds of atoms in the world. These 100 atoms combine in different ways to make all matter in the world.

The ten most common kinds of atoms in the world are oxygen (O), silicon (Si), aluminum (Al), iron (Fe) calcium (Ca), sodium (Na), potassium (K), and magnesium (Mg). These are elements. Atoms of different elements combine to make compounds. A *compound* consists of different elements.

Atoms are very tiny. Scientists can see them with an electron microscope, and they study atoms in other ways too. An atom has two main parts: the nucleus and electrons. The *nucleus* is the center of the atom. *Electrons* are tiny parts that go around the nucleus. The nucleus also has two parts: *protons* and *neutrons*. There are the same number of protons in the nucleus as there are electrons in the atom. Electrons, protons, and neutrons, then, are the three parts of an atom.

Parts of the atom have electrical charges. Protons have a positive (+) electrical charge; neutrons have no electrical charge; and electrons have a negative (−) charge. In an atom, there are the same number of protons and electrons. Therefore, the positive protons balance the negative electrons, and an atom is electrically neutral.

All atoms contain protons, neutrons, and electrons. Different atoms have different numbers of these particles. For example, aluminum has thirteen electrons, thirteen protons, and fourteen neutrons. Iron has twenty-six protons, twenty-six electrons and thirty neutrons.

Scientists divide matter into its smallest parts. Atoms are small parts of matter. They are made up of electrons, protons, and neutrons. Scientists study atoms to learn more about matter.

447 words _________ time _________ wpm

MAIN IDEA

Choose the main idea.

a. An atom is electrically neutral.

b. Scientists divide matter into elements and atoms.

c. Atoms of elements combine to make molecules of compounds.

d. The number of protons in an atom is the atomic number.

COMPREHENSION QUESTIONS

Write **T** before true statements and **F** before false statements. Do not look back at the reading.

_______ 1. Atoms are small parts of matter.

_______ 2. Protons, neutrons, and electrons are parts of atoms.

_______ 3. Scientists divide matter into smaller and smaller parts.

_______ 4. A molecule of sugar is not sugar.

_______ 5. Oxygen is an element.

_______ 6. Protons and electrons are part of the nucleus of an atom.

_______ 7. Protons have negative electrical charges.

_______ 8. Light and heat are forms of energy.

_______ 9. *Scientists cannot study atoms, because they are too small.

_______ 10. *An atom has no electrical charge.

_______ number answered correctly

After correcting your answers, go back to the article and find out the reason for the correct answers. Try to understand the new words in the context.

Write the line number of the sentence that states the main idea of this article. _________

Write the line number of the sentence or sentences that support your answer to questions 9 _________ and 10 _________.

VOCABULARY IN CONTEXT

Find these words in the text. The line number is in parentheses. Write a definition from the text.

1. matter (2) ______________________
2. molecule (8) ______________________
3. atom (13) ______________________
4. element (21) ______________________
5. compound (22) ______________________
6. nucleus (26) ______________________
7. electron (27) ______________________
8. proton (28) ______________________
9. neutron (28) ______________________

ADDITIONAL READING

Read the following paragraphs about atomic number and atomic weight. Solve the problems that follow.

Atomic Number and Atomic Weight

The *atomic number* of an atom is the number of protons in the atom. Hydrogen (H) has only one proton; it is the simplest atom. Uranium (U) is the most complex atom; it has 92 protons. The atomic number of hydrogen is 1, and the atomic number of uranium is 92.

The *atomic weight* of an atom is the total number of neutrons and protons. Hydrogen (H) has one proton and no neutrons; therefore, its atomic weight is 1. The atomic weight of uranium is 238; it contains 92 protons and 146 neutrons.

The number of protons in the nucleus of an element is the atomic number. Each element has a different atomic number. The atomic weight is the number of protons plus the number of neutrons. Scientists write the atomic number before the symbol of the element and the atomic weight after the symbol.

Problems to Solve

1. Look at the diagram of an oxygen (O) atom, and answer the questions.

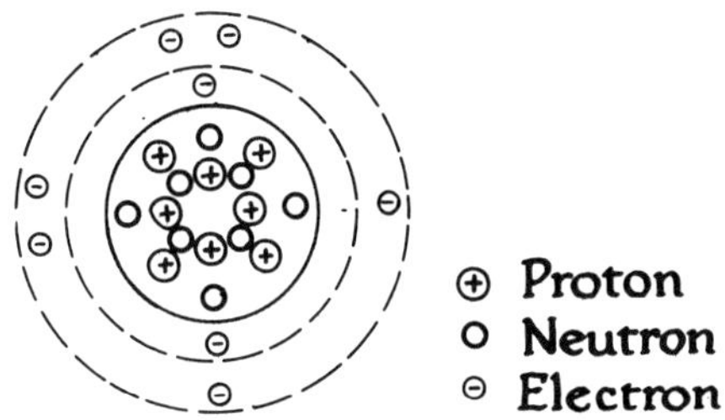

   a. How many protons are there?
   b. How many electrons are there?
   c. How many neutrons are there?
   d. What is the atomic number?
   e. What is the atomic weight?

2. The atomic number of chromium (Cr) is 24. The atomic weight is 52.
   a. How many protons are there in chromium?
   b. How many neutrons are there?

3. Look at the diagram of aluminum (Al). Answer these questions.

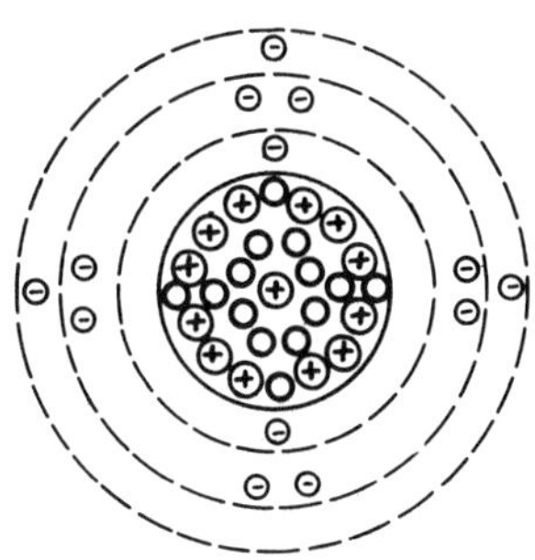

   a. How many protons are there?
   b. How many neutrons are there?
   c. How many electrons are there?
   d. What is the atomic weight?
   e. What is the atomic number?

lesson 11

Isotopes

preview Before you read, look at the diagram of three different hydrogen atoms. How are they different? Read the article and find out.

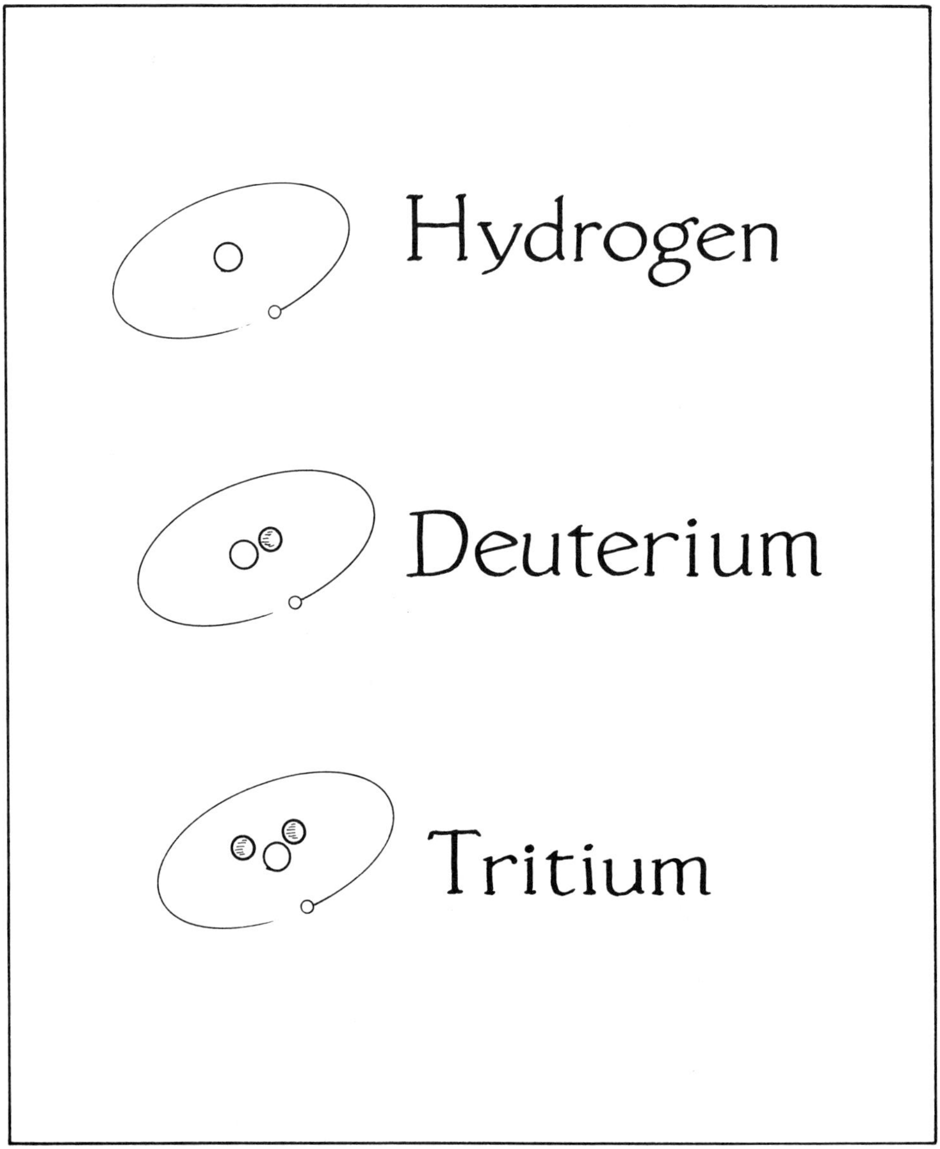

Isotopes are atoms of the same element. They have different atomic weight, or *mass*. All atoms of the same element have the same number of protons and electrons, but isotopes do not have the same number of neutrons. Some elements have only one isotope. For example, aluminum (Al) and gold (Ag) each have only one isotope. Other elements, such as tin (Sn) or hydrogen (H) have several isotopes.

Hydrogen has three isotopes: protium, deuterium, and tritium. Light hydrogen or protium has a mass number of 1 because the nucleus of protium has only one particle: the proton. Deuterium has a mass number of 2 because the nucleus has two particles: one proton and one neutron. The neutron has almost the same mass as the proton. Tritium has a mass number of 3 because its nucleus has three particles: one proton and two neutrons.

Uranium also has several isotopes. One isotope of uranium has a mass weight of 235, and another has a mass weight of 238. Scientists write them like this: 92-U-235 and 92-U-238. All isotopes of uranium have ninety-two protons, so scientists often write only U-235 and U-238.

Some isotopes are *radioactive*. A radioactive isotope loses or gives off particles from its nucleus. It decays. It loses particles and becomes lighter in weight. For example, U-238 and U-235 are radioactive. They decay into lighter isotopes, and finally they become *stable* isotopes of lead (Pb). A stable isotope does not decay or lose particles from its nucleus. It does not change. Many elements have stable isotopes. They are not radioactive.

There are many uses for radioactive isotopes. For example, archaeologists use radioactive carbon to learn how old things are. Scientists use U-235 for atomic bombs and nuclear reactors.

Biochemists use radioactive carbon to study photosynthesis in green plants. Doctors use radioisotopes to study and take care of some illnesses. Radioisotopes are very useful.

325 words ________ time ________ wpm

MAIN IDEA

Choose one main idea for this article.

a. Hydrogen and uranium have several isotopes.

b. Isotopes of an element have different masses.

c. Some isotopes are radioactive.

d. Hydrogen has three isotopes.

COMPREHENSION QUESTIONS

Write **T** before true statements and **F** before false statements. Do not look back at the reading.

_______ 1. Isotopes of the same element have different numbers of protons.

_______ 2. A radioactive isotope decays or loses particles from its nucleus.

_______ 3. All elements have more than one isotope.

_______ 4. Radioactive isotopes are not very useful.

_______ 5. Protium, deuterium, and tritium are isotopes of hydrogen.

_______ 6. All elements are radioactive.

_______ 7. U-235 and U-238 are different elements.

_______ 8. Protons and neutrons are particles.

_______ 9. Stable isotopes decay or lose particles.

_______ 10. *H-1, H-2, and H-3 are the three isotopes of hydrogen.

_______ number answered correctly

After correcting your answers go back to the article to find out why the answers are correct. Try to understand the words in context.

Write the line number of the sentence that states the main idea of this article. _________

Write the line number of the sentence or sentences that support your answer to question 10 _________.

OUTLINE

This article has three parts. Answer the questions to complete the outline.

I. What are two examples of elements that have isotopes?

A. ____

B. ____

II. What are two kinds of isotopes?

A. ____________________

B. ____________________

III. What are some uses of radioisotopes?

A. ____________________

B. ____________________

C. ____________________

D. ____________________

ADDITIONAL READING

Read the following paragraph about carbon-14 dating. Then write the main idea in one sentence.

Carbon-14 Dating

There are many uses for radioactive carbon (C-14). One important use is in archaeology. Archaeologists use radioactive carbon to discover the age of ancient plants. C-14 comes from the sun and is found in all living things. Archaeologists can calculate the age of plants that lived in the past because radioisotopes decay at the same rate. The rate of decay is called the *half-life*. The half-life is the time necessary for half of the atoms to decay. Radioactive carbon (C-14) has a half-life of 5,730 years. That means that after 5,730 years, half of the radiocarbon atoms remain; one half of the radioactive atoms are still in the sample. After 11,460 years, one-fourth of the atoms are still in the sample, and after 17,220 years one-eighth of the atoms remain. Archaeologists can measure the number of radioactive atoms and discover the age of ancient plant material.

lesson
12

Electromagnetic Waves

preview Before you begin to read, look at the electromagnetic spectrum in the illustration. Read the article to find out about electromagnetic waves other than visible light.

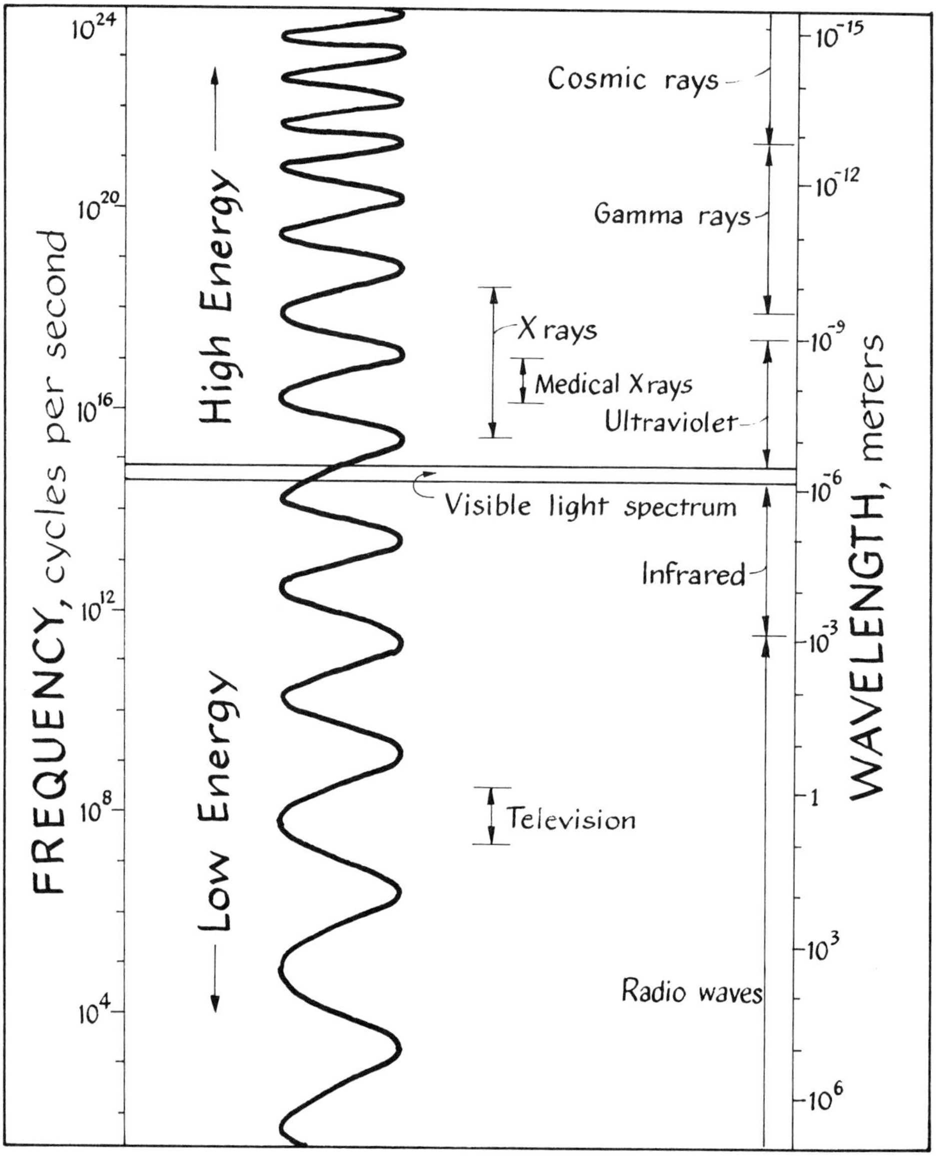

There are many kinds of electromagnetic waves. X-rays and microwaves are two kinds. These waves come from many sources. The sun produces almost all kinds of electromagnetic waves. Changes in atoms and their nuclei also produce electromagnetic waves. All kinds of electromagnetic waves are part of the electromagnetic spectrum.

Different kinds of electromagnetic waves have different wavelengths and different frequencies. *Wavelength* is the distance from a point on one wave to the same point on the next wave. The number of waves from the source in one second is the *wave frequency*. Short waves have a high frequency because there are more waves in one second. Short waves also have more energy. Long waves have a low frequency because there are few waves in one second.

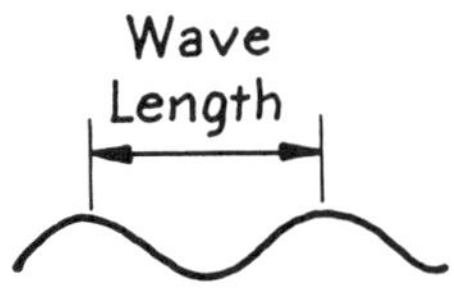

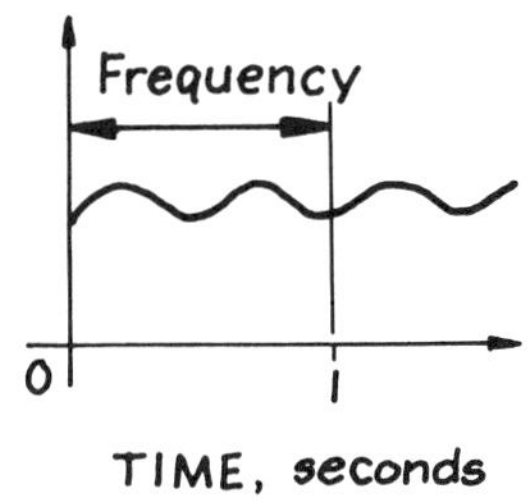

Light

VISIBLE LIGHT Visible light waves are the only electromagnetic waves that we can see. Light comes from many sources: the sun, electric lights, fire. Light is necessary for all life on earth because without light there is no photosynthesis. In 1666, Sir Isaac Newton discovered the visible spectrum of light. He put a glass prism—a three-sided piece of glass shaped like a pyramid—in front of a light. He saw a rainbow of colors: red, orange, yellow, green, blue, indigo, and violet. Scientists now know that the different colors of the spectrum have different wavelength and frequencies.

Newton thought that light was made of very tiny particles. He called them *corpuscles*. Scientists today know that all electromagnetic waves are made of tiny particles that travel like waves. These tiny particles are called *photons*.

INFRARED LIGHT Infrared light rays are invisible. We cannot see them, but Sir William Herschel discovered them in 1800 when he was measuring heat from the visible light spectrum. There was a lot of heat below the red in the visible spectrum. *Infra* means "below" in Latin, so he called these rays *infrared* or "below the red." Infrared waves give heat, and people use them for cooking either on a fire or in an oven. Photographers also use infrared cameras. An infrared camera can take pictures in the dark because it can "see" heat.

ULTRAVIOLET LIGHT Ultraviolet light is also invisible. *Ultra* in Latin means "beyond." Ultraviolet light is after the violet color in the visible light spectrum. Ultraviolet waves have a higher frequency than visible light rays. These rays cause sunburn when we stay in the sun too long. They are useful in medicine because they kill microscopic organisms that cause disease. Fluorescent lights also use ultraviolet waves.

Radio Waves

LONG AND SHORT WAVES Other electromagnetic waves carry pictures and sounds. Radio waves are the longest electromagnetic waves, and they have the lowest frequency. Some radio waves can be many miles or kilometers long. They are beyond the infrared waves on the electromagnetic spectrum. Short radio waves are used in shortwave radios. They carry messages for short distances. Longer radio waves are used in regular radio broadcasts.

MICROWAVES The shortest radio waves are microwaves. *Micro* in Latin means "small." Microwaves are used in radar. Radar helps airplanes fly in darkness at night and in bad weather. Microwaves are also used in medicine, industry, and cooking. They can cook food very quickly.

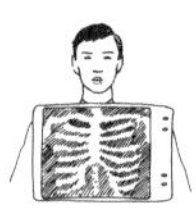

Radioactive Waves

X-RAYS In 1895, Wilhelm Konrad Roentgen discovered X-rays. He called them X-rays because he did not know what they were. In medicine the science of X-rays is called roentgenology. X-ray wavelengths are shorter than ultraviolet rays; they have a higher frequency, and they are beyond the ultraviolet on the electomagnetic spectrum. Many different medical instruments use X-rays to allow doctors to "see" inside the body. These X-ray machines are very useful, but doctors and patients have to be careful with X-rays. They can also harm the body. X-rays hurt living cells.

GAMMA RAYS Gamma rays are more powerful than X-rays. They have more energy. They are shorter in length and have a higher frequency. They come from radioactive material such as uranium (U) and radium (Ra). When radioactive atoms decay, the nuclei break into pieces and lose energy. The energy leaves the nucleus in the form of gamma ray photons. These photons can kill and destroy all living cells. They can destroy, but they are also useful. Doctors use radioactive radium to treat diseases such as cancer. Gamma rays kill the cancer cells. Gamma rays also make the faces of watches and clocks glow in the dark.

Electromagnetic waves are very useful in medicine, industry, and in our houses in everyday life. In fact, some electromagnetic waves are necessary for life. We need energy from the sun to live. On the other hand, electromagnetic rays can be dangerous. Ultraviolet rays from the sun can seriously burn the skin, and radioactive rays from nuclear changes can destroy the world.

789 words ________ time ________ wpm

Electromagnetic Waves, Robert Irving, Alfred A. Knopf: New York, 1960 (juvenile).
Rays and Radiation, Robert Scharff, G. P. Putnam's Sons, New York, 1960 (juvenile).

MAIN IDEA

Choose the main idea of this article.

a. There are many electromagnetic waves and they are both useful and dangerous.

b. X-rays are the most useful electromagnetic waves, but they are dangerous.

c. Light is the only electromagnetic wave that we can see.

d. Electromagnetic waves are very dangerous.

COMPREHENSION QUESTIONS

Mark the following statements **T** (true) or **F** (false). Do not look back at the article.

_______ 1. Electromagnetic waves do not come from the sun.

_______ 2. Electromagnetic waves come from changes in atoms and their nuclei.

_______ 3. All electromagnetic waves are the same.

_______ 4. Electromagnetic waves are not very useful.

_______ 5. They are sometimes very dangerous.

_______ 6. Electromagnetic waves have lengths and frequencies.

_______ 7. We can see infrared and ultraviolet light.

_______ 8. The shortest radio waves are microwaves.

_______ 9. Radioactive waves can kill living cells.

_______ 10. Radioactive waves can destroy the world.

_______ 11. *Microwaves are used in many fields.

_______ 12. *Radio waves are longer than visible light.

_______ number answered correctly

After correcting your answers, go back to the article to find out why they are correct. Try to understand new words in context.

Write the line number of the sentence that states the main idea of this article. _________

Write the line number of the sentence or sentences that support your answer to questions 11 _________ and 12 _________.

VOCABULARY IN CONTEXT

Match the new word from the lesson with its definition. The line number is in parentheses. Do not use your dictionary. Reread the text if necessary.

_______	1. source (2)	a.	where something comes from
_______	2. produce (3)	b.	to give or to make
_______	3. nuclei (4)	c.	we cannot see it
_______	4. visible (14)	d.	to find for the first time
_______	5. discover (17)	e.	plural of nucleus
_______	6. invisible (27)	f.	we can see it
_______	7. powerful (63)	g.	strong; has much energy
_______	8. destroy (77)	h.	kill

ROOTS AND PREFIXES

Look at these words from this article. What do you think *vis* means? What do you think *in* means?

visible	can see it
invisible	cannot see it

These are the roots, prefixes, and suffixes that you have studied. Match them with their meanings.

_______	1. a	a. plant
_______	2. annu	b. the same
_______	3. bi	c. two
_______	4. bio	d. ten
_______	5. bot	e. away
_______	6. cent	f. year
_______	7. dec	g. across
_______	8. dia	h. one hundred
_______	9. equi	i. life
_______	10. ex, exo	j. inside
_______	11. in	k. out of
_______	12. in	l. person who
_______	13. ist	m. not
_______	14. later	n. small
_______	15. nom	o. measure
_______	16. metr	p. side
_______	17. micro	q. name
_______	18. migr	r. move

_______	1. mille	a. many
_______	2. miss	b. light
_______	3. multi	c. again
_______	4. oct	d. one thousand
_______	5. ology	e. eight
_______	6. photo	f. four
_______	7. quad	g. send
_______	8. re	h. study of
_______	9. scope	i. half
_______	10. semi	j. see

______	11. therm	k.	across
______	12. trans	l.	animal
______	13. tri	m.	heat
______	14. uni	n.	three
______	15. vert	o.	one
______	16. zoo	p.	turn

Read these sentences and answer the questions.

1. His *vision* is not very good. Does he need glasses to see better?
2. Microscopic organisms are *invisible* to the human eye. Can the human eye see them without a microscope?
3. Mr. Kennedy is a *botanist*. What does he study?
4. Do *biochemists* study the chemistry of living or nonliving things.
5. There are many *migrant* workers in Arizona. Do they work in the same place all the time?
6. The tuition for the university is $2,400 *annually*. How often do students pay the $2,400?
7. Some diseases are caused by unidentified *microbes*. What do you think a microbe is?
8. Her cousin was a semifinalist in the national music contest. Did the cousin take first place?
9. Which insect has more legs: a centipede or a millipede?
10. The revolutionary was *exiled* from the country. Did he stay in the country or go outside the country?
11. That exercise is *impossible*. Is it possible to do it?
12. The two countries signed a *bilateral* agreement. Did both sides agree?
13. My best friend is *trilingual*. How many languages does she speak?
14. The thirteen original colonies *united* to form the United States. Did the colonies form one country?
15. I need to *transplant* some flowers in my garden. Am I going to plant new flowers or move old flowers?

chapter

3

Business

lesson 13

Banking Services

preview Read this article to find out the different services offered by most banks in the United States.

Photo provided by Valley National Bank

Everyone needs money to buy food, clothes, and housing. Very few people can produce everything that they need. Today, most people use money to buy these things. Buying and selling are necessary for living. Money is an important part of life, and banks control the money in most places. In the United States, there are many different banks, and they offer many different services.

The most common banking service is the *checking account*. People deposit, or put, their money in the bank, and then they can write *checks* to buy things. A check is a piece of paper. It tells the bank to pay the seller. The bank must pay the seller from the customer's account. The customer usually pays the bank a *service charge* for a checking account. The service charge is sometimes five or eight dollars a month. There is not always a monthly fee, but then customers pay 10 or 20 cents for each check that they write.

Another banking service is the *savings account*. People can deposit some of their money in a savings account. They do not usually need this money right now. They will leave the money in the bank and withdraw it when they need it—next month or next year. Because the money will stay in the bank, the bank can use the money. It will pay interest on the savings account. *Interest* is the money that the bank gives to the customer. For example, imagine that a customer put $3,000 in a savings account on January 1. If the bank pays 5 1/2 percent interest, the customer will have about $3,045 in March. The bank paid $45 in interest for three months.

Loans are another important banking service. A bank can give money to businesses and to individual people. The bank may loan money to a business to buy more machines or tools. For example, a bakery may borrow money from the bank to buy more ovens. The bank may also lend money to individuals. The bank may loan money to someone to buy a car or to buy a house. Some people borrow money from the bank to build swimming pools or to repair their houses. The bank always charges interest on loans. The borrower must repay the loan plus the interest. The interest on loans is always higher than the interest on savings accounts.

Banks in the United States usually have *safe deposit boxes*. These boxes are in the vault at the bank. The *vault* is a room that has a very heavy door with a very safe lock on it. Because it is very difficult to get into the vault of a bank, a safe deposit box is a good place to keep important things. Customers can rent the boxes from the bank for a small fee each year. Many people keep their important papers, such as their birth certificate, marriage certificate, or passport, in their safe deposit boxes. Some people keep gold, silver, and other valuable gems such as diamonds or emeralds in their safe deposit boxes.

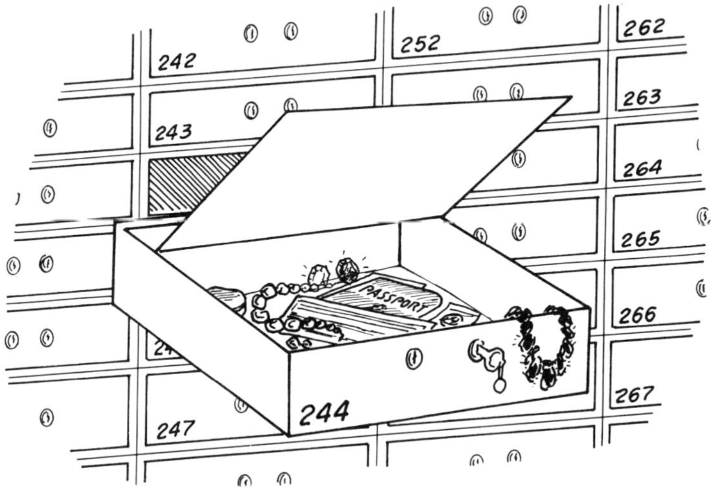

Another important banking service is the *automatic teller machine*. Many banks have bank machines outside the bank so that customers can get their money any time they want it, day or night. Customers can deposit (put money into the bank) or withdraw (take money out of the bank). They can get cash any time—if they have money in their accounts!

Banks control the money. They keep money for people, and they give loans. Banks control the interest rate. In this way, they can control the amount of money for business and individual loans. Banks also offer their customers many useful services, such as savings and checking accounts and loans. In addition, banks try to make using money easier with electronic machines.

631 words ________ time ________ wpm

MAIN IDEA

Choose the main idea of this article.

a. The most important service is a checking account.

b. Banks offer many services to their customers.

c. A safe deposit box is very safe.

d. Everyone needs money.

Which of the following bank services available to bank customers are discussed in the reading? Circle the correct answers. Do not look at the reading.

a. buying and selling

b. savings accounts

c. service charges

d. checking accounts

e. loans

f. building a swimming pool

g. safe deposit boxes

h. valuable jewelry

i. automatic teller machines

COMPREHENSION QUESTION

Write **T** before true statements and **F** before false statements. Do not look back at the reading.

______ 1. Most people need money to buy the things that they need.

_______ 2. Buying and selling is not important for most people.

_______ 3. Some people write checks to buy food and clothes.

_______ 4. Checking accounts are free. People do not need to pay money to the bank for this service.

_______ 5. Banks pay interest on savings accounts.

_______ 6. Banks only loan money to businesses.

_______ 7. Some people borrow money from the bank to buy houses or cars.

_______ 8. Loan customers must pay interest on their loans.

_______ 9. Safe deposit boxes are not a safe place to keep gold and important papers.

_______ 10. Most banks do not offer many services.

_______ number answered correctly

Write the line number of the sentence that states the main idea of this article. _________

USING NEW VOCABULARY

Do this exercise if your score on the comprehension questions was below 7, or if you want to practice the new words. Did you understand the new words and ideas? Go back to the reading and answer these questions. Pay attention to new words, but try not to use the dictionary.

1. Why do people need money?
2. Who controls the money in most places?
3. What is a check?
4. How much is the service charge for a checking account?
5. When do customers need the money in a savings account?
6. Why do businesses borrow money?
7. Why do individuals borrow money?
8. What does the bank charge for loans?
9. Why are safe deposit boxes a good place to keep valuable things?

10. Are safe deposit boxes expensive?
11. What do people keep in their safe deposit boxes?
12. When do customers use bank machines?
13. What three things can customers do at bank machines?
14. What do banks do?

VOCABULARY IN CONTEXT

Read these sentences from the article. Choose the meaning for the *italicized* word.

1. The most common banking *service* is the checking account. Another service is the savings account. Loans are also a banking service.
   a. bank accounts
   b. things banks do for customers
   c. to borrow money from the bank
2. People *deposit*, or put, their money in the bank, and then they can write checks any time.
   a. take money out of the bank
   b. spend the money
   c. put money into the bank
3. Banks offer many services to their *customers*, such as checking and savings accounts.
   a. people who work in the bank
   b. people who use the bank
   c. bank accounts
4. Customers can leave the money in a savings account until they need to *withdraw* it to buy something.
   a. take money out of the bank
   b. borrow money from the bank
   c. put money into the bank
5. The bank may also give someone some money to build a house. In this case, the customer *borrows* money from the bank and must repay the loan plus interest.
   a. deposit money in the bank
   b. use the money from a customer's checking account
   c. use the bank's money

6. Customers usually pay a checking *fee* of five to eight dollars a month to use the checking account.
   a. interest on a loan
   b. money the bank pays the customer
   c. a small amount of money to use or rent something

Find these words in the text. The line numbers are in parentheses. *Do not* use your dictionary, but write a definition *from the text* for these words about banks and banking.

1. checking account (7) ______________________
2. check (8) ______________________
3. service charge (11) ______________________
4. savings account (15) ______________________
5. interest (20) ______________________
6. loan (24) ______________________
7. vault (34) ______________________
8. safe deposit box (33) ______________________
9. automatic teller (42) ______________________

WORD FORMS

In English there are word families. Words in these families are related. Usually they have different suffixes at the end of the word. Sometimes if you can divide a new word into its parts, you will find the meaning. It is important to know the different forms of words. Study the eight word families below. Look at the suffixes. Do the suffixes "-er," "-tion," and "-ance" make nouns, verbs, or adjectives? List four suffixes that make adjectives. Learn these word families.

Verb	*Noun*	*Adjective*
1. deposit	deposit	
	depositor	
2. produce	production	productive
3. differ	difference	different
4. sell	sale	
	seller	

Verb	*Noun*	*Adjective*
5. insure	insurance	
6. value	value	valuable
7. employ	employee	
	employer	
8. use	use	useful
		useless

To fill in each blank below, first decide what kind of word is necessary. Then find the correct word in the list above. Use words from family 1 in sentence 1, words from family 2 in sentence 2, and so on. Fill in the blanks with the correct form of the word.

1. The worker ______________ his paycheck in the checking account every two weeks.
2. That company ______________ pencils.
3. What is the ______________ between a checking account and a savings account?
4. I bought these tennis shoes on ______________.
5. Most people have car ______________.
6. People keep their ______________ papers and jewelry in a safe deposit box.
7. Large companies such as IBM ______________ thousands of people.
8. Banks offer many ______________ services.

ADDITIONAL READING

Read about Electronic Funds Transfer (EFT), then list four advantages of it.

Electronic Funds Transfer

In the future, machines will take the place of many bank tellers. A new system, *electronic funds transfer (EFT)*, allows the bank or the customer to move money from one account to another. For example, a worker receives her monthly paycheck, her salary. Her employer, the company that she works for, can deposit her salary into her checking account directly. She does not have to go to the bank. Her bank can also pay her monthly bills: the telephone, the water, the gas, and the electricity. It will also be possible for her to pay for food at the supermarket by EFT. The supermarket will automatically withdraw money from her account at the bank to pay for the food that she buys.

Some employers already deposit their employees' checks in the bank directly. Maybe, in the future, people will not carry money, and machines will pay for everything.

List four advantages of EFT.

1. ______________________________
2. ______________________________
3. ______________________________
4. ______________________________

Balancing a Check Book

This is an example of a check register. It is a record of the checks from my checking account. Fill in the balance.

Check Number	Date	Pay To	Deposit	Check or withdrawal	Balance
					Balance Forward 74.68
2300	4/20	Exxon—gas for the car		9.75	
2301	4/20	Safeway—groceries		42.34	
2302	4/24	Pizza Hut—dinner		14.94	
	4/28	deposit	409.32		
2303	4/28	telephone company		15.07	
2304	4/28	electric company		35.49	
2305	4/28	water company		18.37	
2306	4/28	rent		175.00	
2307	4/28	cable TV		13.02	
	5/1	monthly service charge		4.50	

Nickels, Dimes & Dollars, How Currency Works, R. V. Fodor, William Morrow and Company, New York, 1980 (juvenile).

A Matter of Money: What Do You Do With a Dollar? Ruth Cavin, S. G. Phillips, New York, 1978 (juvenile).

lesson 14

Investments

preview Do you ever have extra money? What do you do with it? Read this article to see what some people do with their extra money.

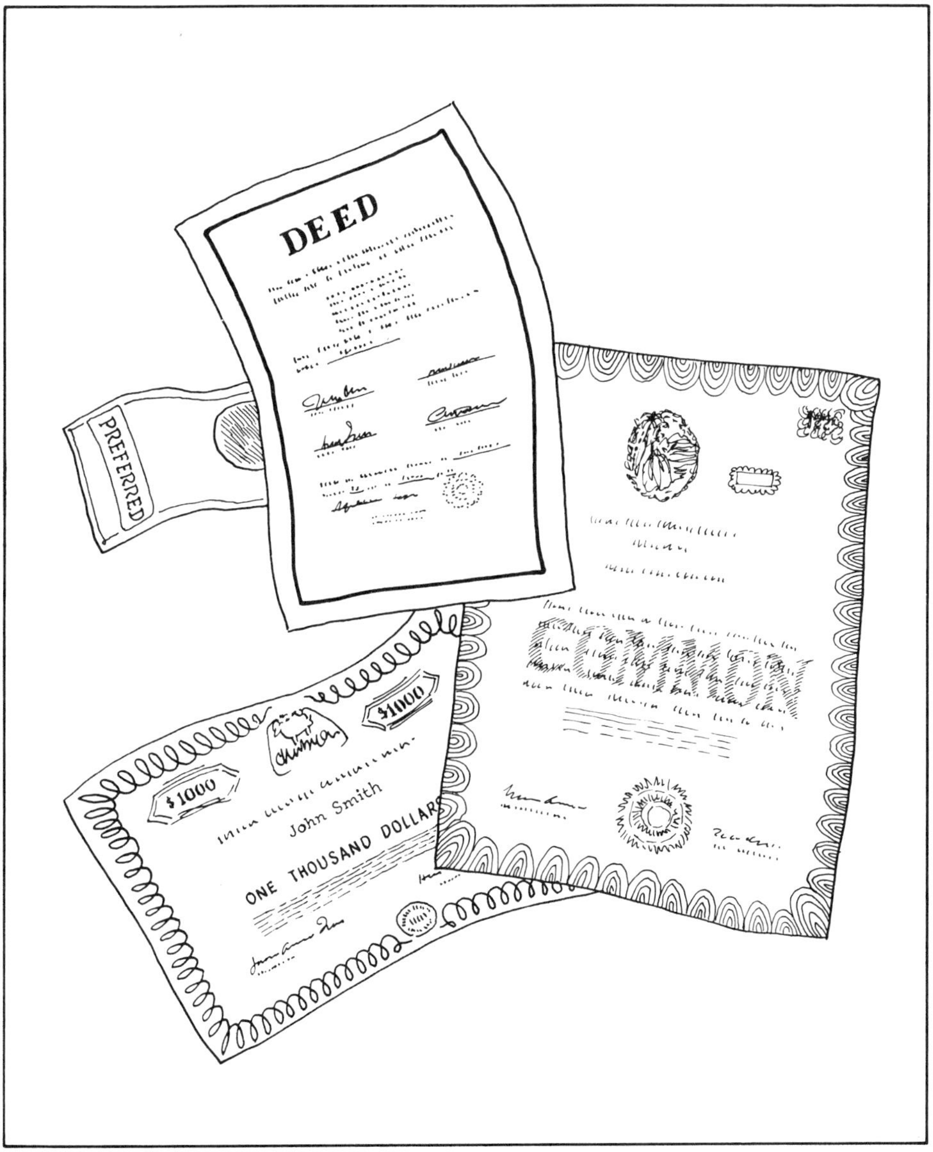

Some people have more money than they need. In the United States, these people want to make more money from their extra money. How can they get *more* money? They invest it. There are many ways to invest money.

The safest place to invest money is at the bank. Banks have savings accounts and other savings plans. The bank pays interest, but it is often a low rate. However, money is safe in most banks.

A bank does not keep the money that customers put in savings accounts. The bank invests the money to make more money for the bank. It might use the money for loans, or it might invest the money in other ways.

Bonds are another investment. Investors can buy government bonds or bonds from a company such as Exxon or General Motors. A bond is a loan from the investor to the borrower. The borrower must repay the loan plus interest. The interest on bonds is usually higher than in savings accounts. For example, the city government wants to build a new highway around the town. The city needs money, so it sells bonds. People buy the bonds, and the city promises to repay the bonds in a certain number of years. The city will also pay interest. Bondholders will receive their money plus the interest.

Another investment is in stocks. A *stock* is a share or part of a company. If a company needs money, it may take a loan from the bank. It may sell bonds, or it may sell some stock. In other words, the company sells a part of itself. The stockholder owns part of the company. People can buy the stocks. Stocks are not as safe as money in the bank or bonds. Buying stocks is risky because the investor does not know if the company will succeed or fail. If a company succeeds, it earns more money. The money that the company earns for itself is called a profit, and the stockholder also earns some profit. If the company fails and loses money, the stockholder loses money, too. Because the investors own part of the company, they might earn more money or lose money. It depends on the success or failure of the company.

Another investment is buying property. Some people buy *real estate:* buildings, houses, or land, because they hope that the value will increase. People sometimes buy art (paintings or sculpture), gold, antiques (very old things), or precious gems (diamonds, emeralds, sapphires, or rubies). The value of all of these things usually increases with time, and investors can then sell them for a lot of money.

Investment is a way to make more money. Some investments are quite safe, but they do not earn a lot of money. Other investments are risky, but they earn much more money.

How will you invest your extra money? Are you a conservative investor (one who plays safe) or a gambler (one who takes risks)?

494 words ________ time ________ wpm

MAIN IDEA

Choose the main idea for this article.

a. Some investments are risky.
b. Money is usually safe in a bank.
c. Many people invest money in stocks.
d. There are many ways to invest money.

COMPREHENSION QUESTIONS

Write **T** before true statements. Write **F** before false statements. *Do not* look back at the article.

______ 1. Some people have more money than they need.
______ 2. Most people want to make more money.
______ 3. *All people invest their extra money.
______ 4. There are not many ways to invest money.
______ 5. Money in savings accounts is not very safe.
______ 6. Money in savings accounts gets very high interest.
______ 7. The government sometimes sells bonds when it needs money.
______ 8. The government does not pay interest on its bonds.
______ 9. Stocks are a part of a company.
______ 10. Stocks are sometimes risky investments.
______ 11. If the company fails, the stockholder gets more money.
______ 12. The value of gold (Au) usually increases over time.
______ 13. All investments are safe.

_______ 14. *Buying property is the best form of investment.

_______ number answered correctly

Write the line number of the sentence that states the main idea of this article. _________

Write the line numbers of the sentence or sentences that support your answer to questions 3 _________ and 14. _________

USING NEW VOCABULARY

Do this exercise if your score on the comprehension questions was below 10 or if you want to practice the new words. Did you understand the new words and ideas? Read the article again and answer these questions. *Do not* use your dictionary?

1. How much money do some people have?
2. What do they want from their extra money?
3. How can people get more money?
4. What does invest mean?
5. Where is the safest place to invest money?
6. How do investors increase their money in savings accounts?
7. What does the bank do with money in savings accounts?
8. How does the bank invest customers' money?
9. From whom can an investor buy bonds?
10. What is a bond?
11. Why did the city government need money?
12. What will the bondholder receive?
13. Who is the bondholder?
14. What is stock?
15. Name three ways a company can get money.
16. Does the stockholder own part of the company?
17. Why are stocks risky?
18. What does the stockholder get if the company is successful?

19. What does the stockholder get if the company fails?
20. Give three examples of real estate.
21. What usually happens to the value of land?
22. What are antiques?
23. Give three examples of gems.
24. What usually happens to the value of these things?
25. What is a gambler?

OUTLINE

List eight different ways of investing money.

1. ______________________________
2. ______________________________
3. ______________________________
4. property
    a. ______________________________
    b. ______________________________
    c. ______________________________
    d. ______________________________

VOCABULARY IN CONTEXT

Read these sentences from the text. Choose the meaning for the italicized word.

1. Some people have more money than they need. They sometimes want to earn more money from this *extra* money.
    a. not enough money
    b. more money than necessary
    c. the right amount of money
2. People sometimes buy real estate, gold, or diamonds because their value usually *increases* in time.
    a. stays the same
    b. becomes less, smaller
    c. becomes more

3. To get money, the city sells bonds and promises to *repay* them in a certain number of years.
   a. sell more bonds
   b. pay the interest
   c. pay back the money

4. Some investments are quite safe; the investor will not lose money. Other investments are *risky*; the investor may lose money.
   a. not a risk
   b. safe
   c. not safe

5. If the company *succeeds*, there is more profit and more money.
   a. do well
   b. lose money
   c. not make profit

6. If the company *fails*, there is no profit and no money.
   a. do well
   b. not do well
   c. make a profit

WORD FORMS

It is important to learn word families. Study the five families below. Are there any new noun suffixes? Adjective suffixes? Sometimes there is more than one noun. One form is the person (for example, the investor); one noun form is the thing (investment) and one is sometimes the idea (investing). Study and learn the forms of these words.

Verb	*Noun*	*Adjective*
1. risk	risk	risky
2. invest	investment	
	investor	
3. succeed	success	successful
4. fail	failure	
5. save	savings	savings
	safety	safe (safer, safest)

Read the sentences. Decide whether you need a noun, a verb, or an adjective. Choose the correct word from the families above. Use words from family 1 in sentence 1, words from the family 2 in sentence 2, and so on. Fill in the blanks with the correct form of the word.

1. Commodities are a very ______________________ investment.
2. Many ______________________ buy stocks of bonds in order to increase their savings.
3. The ______________________ of a new company depends on a lot of hard work.
4. Many small businesses ______________________ in the first year of business.
5. The best way to ______________________ money is to ______________________ a little every month.

ADDITIONAL READING

Read about commodities. Find out what commodities are and how speculators invest in them. Answer the questions.

Investment in Commodities

Another very risky investment is in commodities. They are the materials that companies and businesses use. Some examples of commodities are wheat, corn, coffee, chickens, and copper.

Investors buy large amounts of a commodity and hope that the price increases. They often buy directly from the producer or a farmer before the commodity is produced. There are many things that can affect the supply of a commodity, and, therefore, the price. If the weather is good next year, there will be a lot of corn, and the price will be low. The investor will lose money. If the weather is bad, the corn will be more expensive, and the investor will earn more money. People who invest in commodities are called *speculators*. To speculate means to guess about the future and to take risks. Speculators take many risks when they buy commodities.

1. What are commodities?
2. Why do investors buy commodities?
3. What affects the price of a commodity?
4. If the weather is good, will the speculator earn or lose money? Why?

Nickels, Dimes, & Dollars, How Currency Works, R. V. Fodor, William Morrow and Company, New York, 1980 (juvenile).

A Matter of Money: What Do You Do With a Dollar? Ruth Cavin, S. G. Phillips New York, 1978 (juvenile).

lesson
15

The Stock Market

preview In the last article, you read about stocks and bonds. Read this article to find out about the stock market.

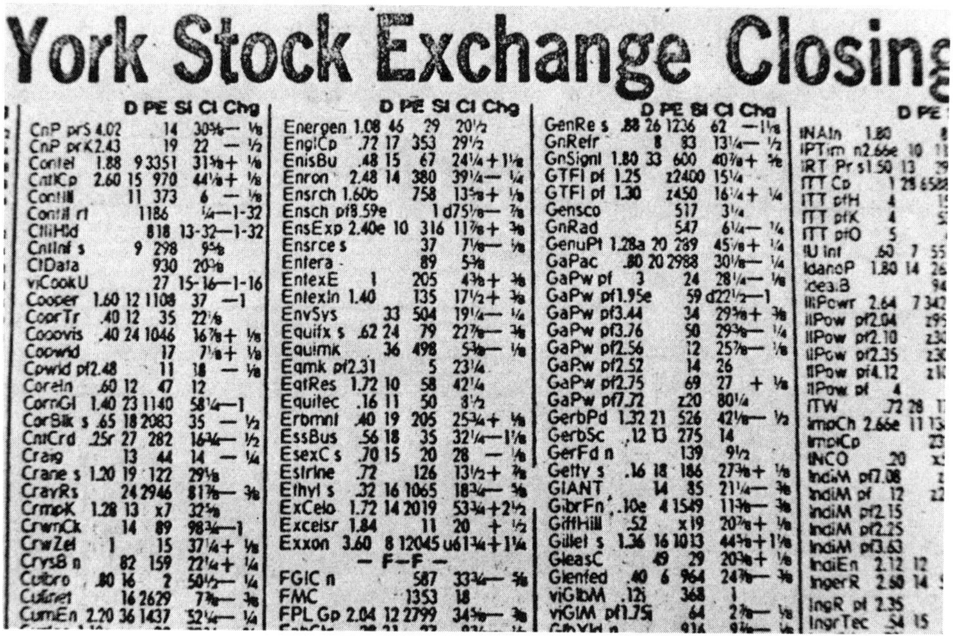
York Stock Exchange Closing

American business gets its capital (money for business) by selling stocks and bonds, or shares of a company. In the United States, the sale of securities (stocks and bonds) takes place mainly on Wall Street in New York City. The New York Stock Exchange and the American Stock Exchange sell stocks and bonds from large companies in the United States. Other important stock exchanges are in Paris, Zurich, and Tokyo, but Wall Street is the financial center of the United States.

Wall Street has been the marketplace for securities since the beginning of United States history. When the first Congress of the United States (1789–1791) needed money, it sold bonds at a market near Wall Street in New York City. Soon many people were buying and selling securities there. In 1792, these merchants built the New York Stock Exchange on the corner of Wall and Broad streets.

Today, 2,000 or 3,000 tourists from all over the world visit the New York Stock Exchange every day. From the visitors' room, they can see the brokers buying and selling securities.

The main purpose of the stock exchanges is to buy and sell securities. In this process, the money that people invest goes to companies that need it for their business. The stock exchanges in New York are the national centers for buying and selling stocks and bonds. If an investor in Tucson, Arizona, wants to buy or sell stocks or bonds, he or she must go to his or her broker. A broker is a person who buys and sells securities. The broker in Tucson calls the broker at the exchange. The broker at the exchange buys or sells the stock. The investor must pay a brokerage fee in addition to the cost of the stock. Some of the large brokerage firms in the United States are Merrill-Lynch, E. G. Edwards, and Prudential-Bache.

People describe the stock market in two ways: a bear market or a bull market. In a bear market, the prices of the stocks are going down, and in a bull market, the prices are going up. Likewise, a bear is an investor who thinks that the prices of the stock will go down. He is a pessimist. A bull is an investor who is an optimist and thinks the prices will go up. Prices of stocks are always changing at the stock exchanges. Brokers all over the United States receive the results immediately by computer. Individual investors can call their brokers or read the price of their stock in the newspaper. Each day the newspaper gives stock prices on the financial page.

Wall Street is the financial center of the United States. The two largest stock markets are there. Investment in the stock market is an investment in American business. The stock market lets investors earn money, and it helps business get the money that it needs. Some investors earn a lot of money in the stock market; other investors lose money. Investors need to know something about stocks and business before they invest. They also need a little luck!

516 words ________ time ________ wpm

MAIN IDEA

Choose the main idea for this article.

a. Wall Street is the financial center of the United States.

b. The stock market is very old.

c. A bear is a pessimist.

d. Many people invest in stocks and bonds.

COMPREHENSION QUESTIONS

Write **T** before true statements. Write **F** before false statements. Answer without looking back at the text.

_____ 1. Wall Street is in New York City.

_____ 2. Securities are stocks and bonds.

_____ 3. Wall Street is a new marketplace, built in the twentieth century.

_____ 4. The first Congress of the United States needed money and sold bonds.

_____ 5. Wall Street is important only to investors; not many tourists visit there.

_____ 6. Brokers buy and sell bonds and stocks.

_____ 7. *Stockbrokers sell stocks and bonds only in New York.

_____ 8. In a bull market, prices go up.

_____ 9. Prices of stocks are always the same.

_____ 10. All investors make money in the stock market.

_____ 11. *Capital is necessary for American business.

_____ 12. *The New York Stock Exchange and the American Stock Exchange sell stocks for American companies.

_____ number answered correctly

After correcting your answers, go back to the reading and try to find out why the answers are correct. Try to understand the vocabulary in context.

Write the line number of the sentence that states the main idea of this article. ________

Write the line numbers of the sentence or sentences that support your answers to questions 7 ________, 11 ________, and 12 ________.

VOCABULARY IN CONTEXT

Read these sentences from the article. Look at the italicized word. Choose the best meaning for it.

1. American business gets its *capital*, money for business, by selling stocks and bonds or shares of a company.
   a. money for business
   b. stocks and bonds
   c. shares
   d. American business
2. In the United States, the sale of *securities* (stocks and bonds) takes place mainly on Wall Street.
   a. Wall Street
   b. stocks and bonds
   c. sales
   d. New York
3. When the first Congress of the United States (1789-1791) needed money, it sold bonds at a *market* near Wall Street in New York City.
   a. place for government
   b. place called Wall Street
   c. place to buy and sell
   d. place to make money
4. Today, 2,000 or 3,000 *tourists* from all over the world visit the New York Stock Exchange every day.
   a. buyers
   b. merchants
   c. brokers
   d. visitors
5. Likewise, a bear is an investor who thinks that the prices of the stock will go down. He is a *pessimist*.
   a. an investor
   b. a negative person
   c. a thinker
   d. an animal

6. A bull is an investor who is an *optimist* and thinks that the prices will go up.
   a. a positive person
   b. a bull
   c. an investor
   d. a thinker
7. Some investors *earn* a lot of money in the stock market; other investors lose money.
   a. make money
   b. lose money
   c. invest money
   d. give money

WORD FORMS

Study these seven word families. Are there any new suffixes? Study and learn the forms of these words.

Verb	*Noun*	*Adjective*
1.	pessimist	pessimistic
	pessimism	
2.	optimist	optimistic
	optimism	
3. finance	finances	financial
4.	nation	national
5. lose	loss	
6. visit	visit	
	visitor	
7. tour	tour	
	tourist	

Fill in the blanks in the sentences below with words from this chart of word families. Fill in sentence 1 with a word from family 1, sentence 2 with a word from family 2, and so on.

1. Don't worry. Charles is a ______________________ person. I'm sure the problem is not as bad as he says.
2. Michael is pleasant to be with. His ______________________ always makes me feel better.
3. The newly married couple needed to borrow money to ____________ their new car.
4. Large brokerage firms have offices all over the ______________________.
5. In 1929, several wealthy people committed suicide because of the ___ of their money.
6. When people are sick, their friends often pay them a ______________ in the hospital.
7. Gail and her family will ______________________ Europe this summer in their new van.

PRONOUN REFERENCE

Pronouns take the place of nouns. When you read, it is important to understand the pronoun. Read these sentences from the article. A pronoun is italicized. Circle the noun that the pronoun repeats. "It" is a pronoun such as "he," "they," "them," "that," and "who," but sometimes "it" is indefinite. It does not repeat a noun. Write "I" if "it" is indefinite in these sentences.

1. When the first Congress of the United States (1789-1791) needed money, *it* sold bonds at a market near Wall Street New York City.
2. Soon many people were buying and selling securities there. In 1792, *these* merchants built the New York Stock Exchange on the corner of Wall and Broad streets.
3. Today 2,000 or 3,000 tourists from all over the world visit the New York Stock Exchange every day. From the visitors' room, *they* can see the brokers buying and selling securities.
4. The stock market lets investors earn money, and *it* helps business get the money that *it* needs.
5. A broker is a person *who* buys and sells securities.
6. In this process, the money *that* people invest goes to companies *that* need the money for *their* buisness.
7. *It* is risky to invest money in commodities.

READING THE FINANCIAL PAGE

Can you read this stock quotation from the newspaper? The explanation below will tell you how to read a stock market report from the financial page in your newspaper.

60⅛ 54½ PepsiCo 1.78 25 7644 58 59⅜ +1⅜

60 1/8	is the highest price for this stock for this year. The price is in dollars. An eighth of 1 dollar is 12 cents. The highest price was $60.12.
54 1/2	is the lowest price paid for this stock this year, $54.50.
PepsiCo	is the name of the company, Pepsi Cola.
1.78	is the last dividend that the stock paid, $1.78 for each share.
25	is the P/E, the price: earnings ratio. If the P/E is high, it shows that the price of the company's stock is low and the profit is high. Investors will want to buy this stock, and the price may go up soon. If the P/E is low, the price of the stock may come down soon because the price is high and the profit is low.
7644	is the number of shares that investors bought and sold this day. Investors bought and sold 764,400 shares of Pepsi Cola stock on this day.
58	is the lowest price for this day, $58.00 for each share.
59 3/8	is the price of this stock when the stock exchange closed for this day, $59.36.
+ 1 3/8	The plus sign after the figure shows that the price was higher than the day before. It was 1 3/8 ($1.36) higher today than yesterday. If today's price is lower than yesterday's there will by a minus sign. (69 3/4 – 1 1/8)

INVESTING IN THE STOCK MARKET

Look at the financial page in your newspaper. Choose four companies that interest you. Write the names of the companies on the chart, and write the closing price each day for one week. Did you make money or lose money?

Don't forget you will have to pay your broker's fee.

Company 1	Company 2	Company 3	Company 4
________	________	________	________
M			
T			
W			
Th			
F			

Do you want to continue for another week? Can you make more money? Can you regain your loss?

Here are the names and abbreviations for some large companies.

Allied Chemical	AlldCh
American Airlines	AmAirlin
Boeing Aircraft	Boeing
Chevron Oil	Chevrn
Dow Chemicals	DowCh
Ford Motor co.	FordM
General Electric Co.	GenEl
International Telephone and Telegraph	IntTT
MacDonald's	MacDonal
Safeway	Safewy
Sony Corp	SonyCp

Nickels, Dimes & Dollars, How Currency Works, R. V. Fodor, William Morrow Company, New York, 1980 (juvenile).

A Matter of Money: What Do You Do with a Dollar? Ruth Cavin, S. G. Phillips New York, 1978 (juvenile).

Wall Street: A Story of Fortunes and Finance, Doris Faber, Harper & Row, Publishers, New York, 1979 (juvenile).

DISCUSSION QUESTIONS

1. Why do people invest money?
2. Do you think the stock market offers good investments?
3. How do you, or how will you, invest money?

lesson
16

Retail Stores

preview What kind of goods do you buy? Where do you go shopping? What kind of store do you shop in? Read this article to find out the different kinds of stores there are in the United States.

Photo provided by AlphaGraphics Printshops of the Future

Buying and selling goods and services is only one part of the marketing process. The marketing process includes thinking of a new product, manufacturing the product, advertising and distributing it, and selling it to the consumer, or buyer. Selling is the last, and an important step in the marketing process.

There are many different ways for the producer of a product to sell the product to the consumer. The producer needs to find the best way to sell the product to the customers.

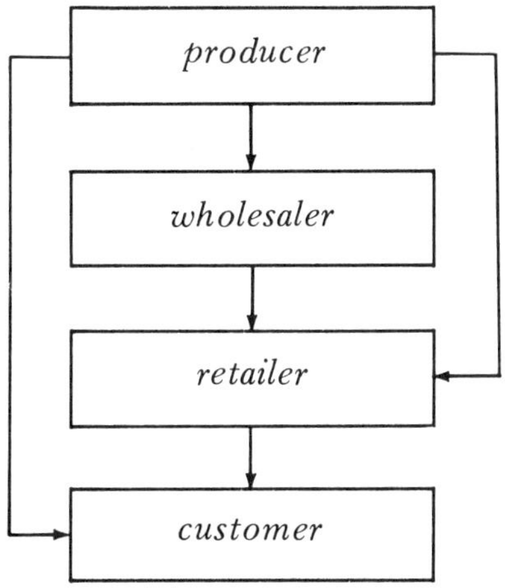

Some companies, such as the Fuller Brush Company, Avon Cosmetics, and Encyclopedia Britannica sell their products directly to the customer. A salesperson comes to the customer's house and shows the product to the customer. Other products such as jewelry, kitchen goods, clothes, and children's toys are also sold in the customer's home at parties. The salesperson helps a customer plan a party. At the party, the salesperson shows the product and invites the guests to buy it. These products are all sold directly to the customer.

Most producers, however, do not sell directly to the customer. They sell to a middleman, who may be either a wholesaler or a retailer. A wholesaler usually buys very large quantities of goods and sells them in large quantities. A wholesaler often sells goods to a retailer, who then sells the goods to the consumer. The difference between a wholesaler and a retailer is their purpose. Wholesale sales are often for the purpose of resale. Occasionally, wholesalers sell large quantities of goods directly to the consumer. Retailers sell directly to the customers for their own use or for family use.

In the United States, many different kinds of retail stores sell goods to the consumer. A few of the common kinds are single-line stores, department stores, supermarkets, discount stores, and convenience markets.

Single-line stores carry one kind, or line, of merchandise. For example, in a sporting goods store, a customer can find all kinds of equipment for sports, such as soccer balls, tennis racquets, and tennis balls. Hardware stores, furniture stores, dress shops, and camera shops are all single-line stores. They carry only one kind of merchandise.

A *department store* is a group of specialty and single-line shops in one large store. Each department, or part, of the store sells a single line of merchandise. There are many departments in one large store. Macy's in New York, Broadway in Los Angeles, Marshall Field in Chicago, and Goldwater's in Phoenix are all large, well-known department stores in the United States.

Department stores sell many different goods, but they do not usually sell food. People often buy their food in large supermarkets. *Supermarkets* are food stores, but they sell many, many other goods besides food. Many supermarkets also sell garden supplies, drugs, books and cards, camera film and supplies, sewing supplies, liquor, small appliances, and other household goods. Some national supermarkets are Safeway, Kroger, Food Fair, and Grand Union.

Discount stores are similar to department stores. They are large, and they sell many different kinds of merchandise. Discount stores offer lower prices but fewer services. They are often self-serve, so there are very few clerks. Customers need to help themselves. The largest discount stores in the United States are K-Mart, Woolco, Target, and Zayre.

Convenience stores are easy to use. They are usually small food stores that carry milk, soft drinks, ice, and other common things that people want in a hurry. They are often open very early in the morning until late at night. They are sometimes open twenty-four hours a day. Seven-Eleven and Circle K are convenience stores.

Like other businesses, retail stores are owned by one person or a large corporation. There can be just one store, or there can be many stores with the same name. Chain stores have the same owner and the same name, and they sell the same goods. Sometimes a small business is very successful, and the owner begins another business in another part of town. The two stores are part of a chain. Later, the owner may have several stores that are part of the same chain. Half of the retail stores in the United States are chain stores, several businesses owned by a single corporation or owner. Safeway is a well-known chain supermarket, and Walgreens is a well-known chain drugstore.

There are many different kinds of retail stores in the United States and many different kinds of ownership. Each producer of goods must decide the best way to sell the goods. A producer may sell a product such as Avon cosmetics directly to the customer in the home. Or the producer may sell the product to a wholesaler, who in turn sells to the retailer. Another producer may sell directly to the retailer. The retailer is the last link of the chain before the consumer. Retail stores may be individually owned, or they may be part of a large chain of several businesses. How to sell a product to the consumer is a major part of the marketing process.

849 words ________ time ________ wpm

MAIN IDEA

Choose the main idea for this article.

a. Selling goods and services is an important part of the marketing process.

b. Some producers sell directly to the consumer.

c. Retailers and wholesalers are middlemen between the producer and consumer.

d. Discount and convenience stores are different kinds of retail stores.

COMPREHENSION QUESTIONS

Write **T** before true statements. Write **F** before false statements. Do not look back at the article.

______ 1. Selling is the only part of the marketing process.

______ 2. Several goods such as jewelry, kitchen goods, and toys are sold at parties in the home of the customer.

______ 3. A wholesaler usually sells directly to the consumer.

______ 4. Wholesalers may sell to a retailer.

______ 5. Department stores usually sell food.

______ 6. Supermarkets sell only food.

______ 7. Discount stores often have lower prices.

______ 8. Chain stores have the same owner but several different outlets or stores.

_______ 9. *Because of large chain stores, you can probably find many of the same stores wherever you go in the United States.

_______ 10. *Consumers buy most of their goods from retailers.

_______ number answered correctly

After correcting your answers, go back to the article to see why the answers were correct. Try to use the context to discover the meaning of new words.

Write the line number of the sentence that states the main idea of this article. _________

Write the line numbers of the sentence or sentences that support your answer to questions 9 _________ and 10 _________.

VOCABULARY IN CONTEXT

Read these sentences from the article. Select the best meaning for the italicized word.

1. The marketing process *includes* new product development, production, advertising, distributing, and selling.
   a. The marketing process is simple and short.
   b. The marketing process doesn't have these parts.
   c. These five things are part of the marketing process.
   d. both a and c
2. *Like* other businesses, retail stores are owned by one person or a large corporation.
   a. the same as
   b. different from
3. Discount stores are *similar to* department stores. They are large and sell many different kinds of merchandise.
   a. different from
   b. exactly the same as
   c. almost the same as

Find these words in the article. The line number is in parenthesis. Write a definition from the text. Do not use your dictionary.

1. wholesaler (18) ______________________
2. retailer (18) ______________________
3. merchandise (30) ______________________
4. single (30) ______________________
5. line (30) ______________________
6. sporting goods store (31) ______________________
7. department (35) ______________________
8. goods (41) ______________________
9. self-serve (50) ______________________

PRONOUN REFERENCE

Read these sentences from the article. Look at the italicized pronoun. Circle the noun that it replaces.

1. At the party, the salesperson shows the product and invites the guests to buy *it*.
2. A wholesaler usually buys very large quantities of goods and sells *them* in large quantities.
3. Convenience stores are easy to use. *They* are usually small food stores *that* carry milk, soft drinks, ice, and other common things *that* people want in a hurry.

PASSIVE

Look at these examples of passive sentences. The passive verb phrase is in italics.

Food *is sold* at Safeway.

Many goods *are sold* at retail stores.

Read the following sentences. Underline the complete passive verb and identify the doer. The doer may be mentioned in the sentence, or you may need to write it. One sentence is not passive.

1. Other products such as jewelry, kitchen goods, clothes, and children's toys are also sold in the customer's home at parties.

2. These products are all sold directly to the customer.
3. Retailers sell directly to the customers for their own use or family use.
4. Like other businesses, retail stores are owned by one person or a large corporation.

SUBJECT-VERB IDENTIFICATION

These sentences are long, with several clauses or phrases. Underline the simple subject and the simple verb of the main sentence. Underline the subject once, and underline the verb twice.

1. Some companies, such as the Fuller Brush Company, Avon Cosmetics, and Encyclopedia Britannica, sell their products directly to the consumer.
2. The difference between a wholesaler and a retailer is their purpose.
3. For example, in a sporting goods store, a customer can find all kinds of equipment for sports, such as soccer balls, tennis racquets, and tennis balls.
4. Each department, or part, of the store sells a single line of merchandise.

ADDITIONAL READING

Read this article about small businesses and franchises. Fill out the outline that follows.

Small Businesses

When consumers want to buy something—food, clothes, furniture, or books—they most often go to a retail store. Retail stores sell directly to the consumer. Many retail stores are small businesses. In the United States, ninety-seven percent of the businesses are small businesses. They are an important part of the marketing process. *Small businesses* are businesses that are small in comparison to large companies. These small businesses earn less than $2 million a year. They are usually owned by an individual or a partnership (two or more people who own the business together). The owner very often manages the business, and there are not many employees.

In the 1960s, a new idea for retail ownership became very popular in the United States. This was the franchise store. The franchise store allows an individual to own and operate a small business with a better chance of success. If someone begins a small business such as a restaurant or a dress shop, it is sometimes difficult to succeed alone. With a franchise, the new owner has the name and the help of a well-known business and is more likely to succeed. Many restaurants are franchise businesses. Some of them are MacDonalds, Burger King, Kentucky Fried Chicken, and Pizza Hut. Each restaurant has a different owner. The owner owns the business, but the company gives the owner the name and the menu and a lot of help with the business. Franchises give owners of small businesses a better chance of success.

Read the first paragraph and list five characteristics of a small business.

1. ______________________________
2. ______________________________
3. ______________________________
4. ______________________________
5. ______________________________

Read the second paragraph and give two advantages of a franchise.

1. ______________________________
2. ______________________________

READING GRAPHS

You may want to start learning to read graphs and charts at this point. If you do, then turn to page 194 and read about bar and circle graphs in chapter 5, lessons 28 and 29.

lesson 17

Ways of Advertising

preview What kind of advertising influences you the most? Why do you buy the products you buy? Do you ever buy something you don't need? Why? Do you buy a brand name product, or do you buy a generic brand? What brands do you prefer? How do you know about new products?

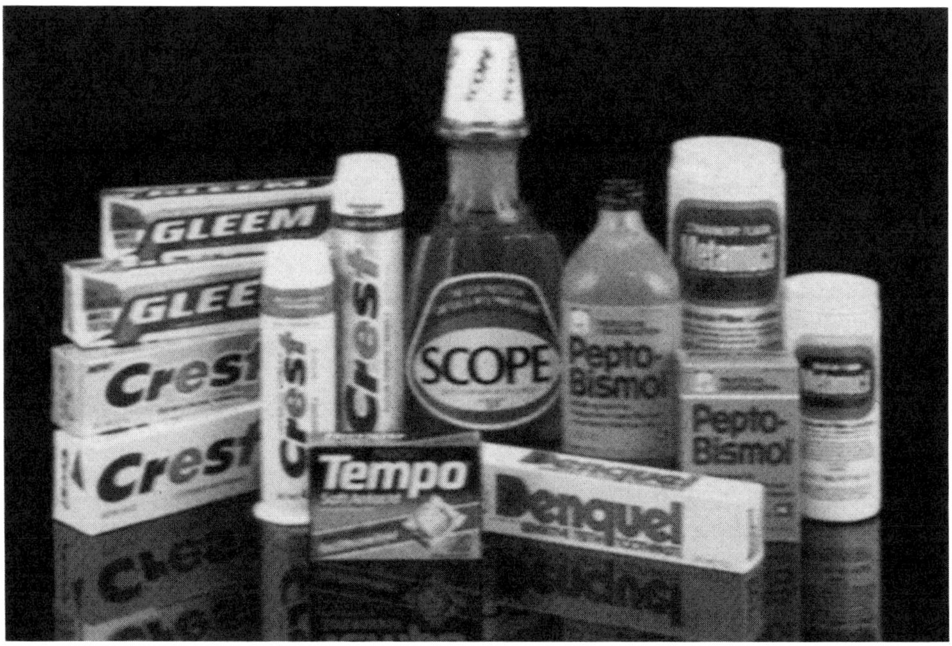

Courtesy of the Proctor and Gamble Company

Advertising is a multibillion dollar business in the United States. More than 33 billion dollars are spent each year for advertising. Advertisements and commercials pay for most television and radio programs. Advertisements also pay for the cost of magazines and newspapers and help sell a product to consumers. It tells about the product. It tells people that the product is better than other products, and it makes the name of the product famous.

Most people see and hear advertising many times every day. Advertisements, or ads, are everywhere. They are in newspapers and magazines; they are on radio and TV; they even come to our mailboxes at home.

Companies or businesses buy space for their ads in newspapers and magazines. They might buy half of a page, one-quarter of a page, or one-eighth of a page. Newspaper ads usually tell customers about sales or special prices in nearby retail stores. Local businesses often advertise in the newspaper because many people in the local area read the paper every day, and the ads may change every day.

Newspapers also have classified ads. Classified ads are a special section of the newspaper. These ads are very small. People advertise things that they want to buy, sell, or rent. Anyone can buy an ad in the classified section.

On radio and TV, advertisers buy time. They may buy a 30-second or a 1-minute commercial. TV time is very expensive, and it is even more expensive on more popular TV and radio shows. A 30-second commercial might cost $150,000, but if 60 million people are watching the program, the cost per person is about 1/4 cent.

Another way to tell the consumer about a product is by direct-mail advertising. Companies mail advertisements to consumers. These ads are in the mailbox almost every day. They are mailed directly to the consumer. If advertisers want to send the ad to everyone in the neighborhood or in the city, they send the ad to "Occupant" or "Resident." This way the ad goes to every house in the area.

Sometimes the advertiser wants to send the ad to a special group of people. Then a mailing list is necessary. Mailing lists are lists of names and addresses of people who might buy the product. They list people by occupation, age, income, or hobbies. Advertisers can buy mailing lists from special companies that prepare them. An advertiser can buy a list of lawyers or a list of all the people with swimming pools, for instance. Advertisers pay for each name. The price may differ from a few cents per name to ten dollars per name.

Advertising tells consumers about a product. If consumers don't know about a product, they cannot buy it. The advertiser must select the

CLASSIFIED
ADVERTISING
CLASSIFIED INDEX & ADVERTISING INFO
EMPLOYMENT
DRIVE TODAY!
$500 DOWN *
Travel Trailers and Campers 720
Bicycles-Gocarts 752
Motorcycle-Offroad 764
Tires 806
Pickups 814
ANNOUNCEMENTS
Business/Financial
MOBILE LIVING
EMPLOYMENT
REAL ESTATE
Employment Opportunities 355
Heavy Equipment 500
Musical Instruments
Farm-Ranch Equipment 526
RESTAURANT
MARKETING COORDINATOR
TAILORS
CLASSIC CAR SOUNDS
7 SALES PROFESSIONALS
APPLIANCE SALESPERSON
RECOVERY CENTERS OF AMERICA
6930 WEICKER
P.O. BOX 160
VELARDE, NM 87582
TEACHER MUSIC
SAM DOTY EQUIPMENT
WATER STORAGE TANKS
TECHNICAL WRITER

best medium—newspaper, TV, radio, direct mail, or mailing lists—to carry the ad to the most people at the lowest cost.

482 words ________ time ________ wpm

MAIN IDEA

Choose the main idea of this article. All of the sentences may be correct, but one is more important than the others. Do not look back at the article.

a. TV time is very expensive for advertisers to buy.

b. Newspapers and magazines are two media for advertising.

c. Every day, $1.55 per person is spent on advertising.

d. Advertising tells consumers about a product.

This article tells about different kinds of advertising. List five different ways to reach the consumer.

1. ____

2. ____

3. ____

4. ____

5. ____

COMPREHENSION QUESTIONS

Write **T** before true statements. Write **F** before false statements. *Do not* look back at the reading.

______ 1. Advertising tells people about a product.

______ 2. TV and radio are the only media that have advertisements.

______ 3. Local businesses often advertise in the local newspapers because these ads can change often and local people can read them.

______ 4. *Individuals as well as businesses place ads in the classified section.

_______ 5. It is very expensive to buy advertising time on TV.

_______ 6. *TV advertising may be one of the cheaper forms of advertising per person.

_______ 7. Advertisers buy mailing lists with names of people who have common interests.

_______ 8. An ad addressed to "Occupant" or "Resident" has come from a mailing list.

_______ 9. *Mailing lists are the cheapest form of advertising.

_______ 10. *Advertising is an important part of business.

_______ number answered correctly

After correcting your answers, go back to the reading to find out why the answers are correct. Try to use the context to discover the meanings of new words.

Write the line number of the sentence that states the main idea of this article. _________

Write the line numbers of the sentence or sentences that support your answer to questions 4 _________, 6 _________, 9 _________, and 10 _________.

WORD FORMS

Study and learn these four word families. What is the difference between different nouns in the same family?

Verb	*Noun*	*Adjective*
1. advertise	advertisement	
	advertising	
2. consume	consumer	
3. produce	producer	
	production	productive
	product	
4.	convenience	convenient

Fill in the blanks in the sentences below with the correct form of the word in the chart. Use a word from family 1 in sentence 1, a word from family 2 in sentence 2, and so on.

1. ________________________ pays for two-thirds of the cost of a newspaper. Large national companies ________________________ on national TV. Michael Jackson made a famous ________________________ for Coca Cola.
2. A________________________ would not know about a new product if there were no ads.
3. That factory is very ____________________; it ____________________ more goods per hour than many others. It is a large ________________ of tires.
4. People shop at Circle K stores because the stores are ________________.

PRONOUN REFERENCE

Read this sentence from the article. Look at the italicized pronouns. Circle the nouns that they replace.

1. Mailing lists are lists of names and addresses of people *who* might buy the product. Advertisers buy *these* from special companies *that* prepare *them*.

PASSIVE

These sentences from the article are passive. Underline the complete verb and identify the doer of the action.

1. Thirty-three billion dollars are spent each year for advertising.
2. Many kinds of media are used to advertise a product.
3. The advertisements are mailed directly to the consumer.

SUBJECT-VERB IDENTIFICATION

These sentences from the article are long, and they have many clauses and phrases. Underline the simple subject and simple verb. Underline the subject once and the verb twice.

1. On TV and radio, commercials pay the total cost of a commercial television or radio program.

2. Local businesses often advertise in the newspaper because many people in the area read the paper every day.
3. If advertisers want to send the ad to everyone in the neighborhood or in the city, they address the ad to "Occupant" or "Resident."
4. Another way to tell the consumer about a product is to use direct mail advertising.
5. If consumers don't know about a product, they can't buy it.

ADDITIONAL READING

Read the article about research in advertising and fill in the outline that follows.

Research in Advertising

In the ad agency, the account manager is in charge of creating an ad. There are several steps in making an ad. These steps include research, planning, and production. Before the account manager can begin to plan an ad, many kinds of research must be done. Marketing researchers study sales patterns. They try to answer the question "Who will buy this product?" Product researchers try to answer the question "Does the customer like this product?" Motivational researchers try to answer the question "Why do the customers buy this product?" This is a difficult question to answer because people sometimes don't tell the real reason why they buy something. Sometimes they don't even know why they bought it. Media researchers look for the answer to the question "Who is watching TV now?" One very famous company that does media research is the Nielsen company. It produces the Nielsen ratings for TV. Each year it tells us which programs are watched by the most people.

When the account manager can answer all these questions, he is ready to plan the ad. He will use all the information to plan a successful ad. He will study the different media very carefully and decide which medium will carry the message the best. He wants to tell the most people for the smallest price. Research about why and what people buy is very important to the account manager.

List four different questions that advertisers ask during their research.

1. ____
2. ____

3. ______________________________________

4. ______________________________________

Discussion Questions

1. Is advertising an important part of business, or is it another form of "brainwashing"?
2. How do different ads attempt to persuade customers to buy a product?
3. Do you buy goods because of advertising?

READING GRAPHS

If you wish to read more graphs, turn to page 203 and do chapter 5, lessons 30 and 31, Line Graphs and Combination Graphs.

lesson 18

Insurance

preview If someone is hurt in your house, are you responsible for his or her medical costs? If you are hurt in the supermarket, will the supermarket pay your medical costs? Read this article to find out how individuals and businesses protect themselves from financial loss.

Individuals and businesses face risk every day. Risk is the danger of losing something. There is a risk of losing life or losing money. For example, individuals are at risk whenever they drive a car. In a car accident, there can be many losses. The driver's car may be damaged; another car may be damaged; a driver or passenger may be injured or killed. Drivers can do two important things to reduce the risk of a car accident. First, they can drive carefully and safely. Also they can be sure their car is in good condition. However, even if the driver is very careful and the car is in very good repair, there is still the risk of an accident. A driver may be injured or the car damaged in an accident. Someone needs to pay for these damages. If the driver has insurance, the insurance will pay for some of the loss.

One way people reduce the risk of financial loss from car accidents is to buy insurance. There are three kinds of car insurance, and it is important to buy all three kinds.

1. *Accident and life insurance on the driver.* The insurance company will pay the driver's family if the driver is killed in the car accident. If the driver has a $100,000 life insurance policy, the company will pay the family $100,000 if the driver dies.

2. *Collision insurance.* The insurance company will pay for the damage to the car. The insurance will pay for repairing the car.

3. *Liability insurance.* This insurance will help pay for the expenses of the other car and driver. The police usually decide who caused the accident. That person must pay for the damages. His or her liability insurance will pay for the other person's losses.

Besides collision and liability insurance for cars, there are many other kinds of insurance. The average family can have many insurance policies: life insurance, disability insurance, car insurance, household insurance, and health insurance.

Life insurance pays the family if the insured person dies. Disability pays the family money if the insured person is hurt and is unable to work. This insurance allows the family to continue to bring in the same amount of money if the working person is killed or injured.

Household insurance protects the family against the loss of their house and property. Property includes the house and the things inside the house: furniture, clothes, stereos, and so on. If the house is destroyed by fire or flood, the insurance company will pay for a new house. If a thief breaks into the house and steals the TV set, the insurance company will pay for a new TV. Most homeowners' insurance policies also have liability protection. If a guest falls in the house and is injured, the insurance will pay for the injury.

Another important insurance is health insurance. Many insurance companies pay 80 to 100 percent of the cost of medical care.

All of this insurance is expensive. Not all families can pay for car, disability, household, health, and life insurance.

The loss or injury of a parent, a sudden illness, or a theft or fire can hurt a family very much. Likewise, an accident or injury can cause a small business to fail. Many business risks can be serious enough to close the business. A fire might destroy the business. An employee can make a mistake and cause a lot of damage. If the company sells food, some spoiled or bad food can cause a customer's illness or death. A theft can be large enough to cause the company to go out of business. Therefore, businesses buy insurance to protect themselves from financial loss. Businesses also buy liability insurance. If a customer is injured and if the business is liable, the insurance will pay the customer. Even city governments buy liability insurance to protect themselves from financial loss in case of an accident.

Another kind of liability insurance is professional liability, or malpractice, insurance. Professional people such as doctors, surgeons, lawyers, architects, accountants, and engineers often buy malpractice insurance. Their mistakes can cause death or injury. A doctor may prescribe the wrong medicine for a patient. An engineer's bridge may fall down and kill and injure several people. The doctor and the engineer are liable for injuries that are caused by their errors. Malpractice insurance pays for these injuries. Many doctors and other professional people must pay very large premiums for their professional liability (malpractice) insurance. In addition to families, businesses, and government, professional people buy insurance to protect their financial future.

757 words ________ time ________ wpm

MAIN IDEA

Choose the main idea for this article.

a. Everyone faces risks every day.

b. Doctors and engineers need malpractice insurance.

c. Insurance protects individuals, businesses, and governments from the risk of financial loss.

d. Liability insurance is very important and necessary.

This article talks about different kinds of insurance. List them in this outline.

Car

1. ______________________________
2. ______________________________
3. ______________________________

Individual and business

1. ______________________________
2. ______________________________
3. ______________________________
4. ______________________________
5. ______________________________

Business

1. ______________________________

Professional

1. ______________________________

COMPREHENSION QUESTIONS

Write **T** before true statements. Write **F** before false statements. *Do not* look back at the reading.

______ 1. Only businesses risk financial losses.

______ 2. *A good driver can always avoid accidents by driving carefully.

______ 3. Liability insurance pays for injuries to another person.

______ 4. Life insurance pays the family if the insured person dies.

______ 5. Insurance is not very expensive.

______ 6. Small businesses do not need insurance.

______ 7. *In the United States, the government pays for hospital and medical care.

______ 8. Professional people buy malpractice insurance to protect themselves from accidents caused by their errors.

______ 9. *It is good idea for drivers to have insurance.

______ 10. *All families, governments, and businesses have insurance.

______ number answered correctly

After correcting your answers, go back to the article to see why the answers were correct. Try to understand the meaning of new words from the context.

Write the line number of the sentence that states the main idea of this article. ________

Write the line numbers of the sentence or sentences that support your answer to questions 2 ________, 7 ________, 9 ________, and 10 ________.

VOCABULARY IN CONTEXT

Look at these words from the text. The line number is in parentheses. Match the words with their meanings.

______	1. risk (1)	a. to hurt
______	2. reduce (6)	b. things people own
______	3. injure (10)	c. to take someone else's property
______	4. property (35)	d. danger of losing something
______	5. break into (38)	e. enter illegally
______	6. steal (38)	f. make something smaller

WORD FORMS

Study and learn the forms of these seven word families.

	Verb	*Noun*	*Adjective*
1.	risk	risk, risks	risky
2.	injure	injury, injuries	
3.	insure	insurance	
4.	disable	disability	
5.		liability	liable
6.	protects	protection	protective
7.	destroy	destruction	destructive

Fill in the spaces in the sentences below with the correct form of the word. Use a word from family 1 in sentence 1, a word from family 2 in sentence 2, and so on.

1. Be careful. Don't take any more ______________________ than necessary.
2. The driver died from ______________________ from the accident.
3. With household ________________one can ________________ almost anything valuable: jewelry, stamps, crystal, and more.
4. Not being able to walk is a great ______________________.
5. The city was ______________________ for the accident caused by the city truck.
6. Insurance ______________________ the insured people from financial disaster.
7. Agnes was a very ______________________ hurricane in 1972.

PASSIVE VERBS

These sentences from the article are in the passive. The passive verb may not be in the main clause. Underline the complete verb and identify the doer of the action.

1. The driver's car may be damaged.
2. A driver or passenger may be injured or killed.
3. If the house is destroyed by fire or flood, the insurance company will pay for a new house.
4. The doctor and the engineer are liable for injuries that are caused by their errors.

SUBJECT-VERB IDENTIFICATION

These sentences are long and difficult. They have several dependent clauses. To help you understand them better, underline the simple subject and the simple verb of the main clause. Underline the subject once and the verb twice.

1. However, even if the driver is very careful and the car is in very good repair, there is still risk of an accident.
2. If the company sells food, some spoiled food can cause a customer's illness or death.
3. In addition to families, businesses, and governments, professional people buy insurance to protect their financial future.

ADDITIONAL READINGS

Read this paragraph about the Prudential-Bache Insurance Company. Write one main idea sentence about the paragraph.

Prudential-Bache Insurance Company

Prudential Insurance Company of America is perhaps the largest insurance company in America. Its ad "A piece of the rock" is a well-known ad for life insurance. The Prudential Company began in 1875 with $30,000, and today it has life insurance in force of more than $294 billion dollars. The company does not sell only insurance. It has a great many investments: $14 billion in real estate; 19 billion in government bonds, and $4 billion in common stock. Prudential has 62,000 employees and 46 billion in assets.* Other large, well known companies are Metropolitan (New York), Equitable Life Assurance (New York), and John Hancock Mutual (Boston).

*Hal B. Pickle and Royce L. Abrahamson, *Introduction to Business*, (Santa Monica: Goodyear Publishing Co., 1980), p. 286. © Scott, Foresman and Company.

Write the main idea in one sentence.

____

____

Insurance Premiums and Probability

Insurance is based on probability or odds. The chance of something happening is its *probability*. For example, insurance companies collect statistics which show how many people die at what age each year or how many fires there are each year. The insurance company uses these statistics to calculate insurance premiums. Premiums are the amounts of money that an individual or business pays for insurance protection.

Here is an example of how the company calculates the premiums. It knows that 2 percent of the people who are 50 years old will die next year. If the company insures 1,000 people who are 50 years old, they know that twenty people will die. If the twenty people are insured for $100,000 each, then the company must pay $2,000,000. Therefore, they will charge the 1,000 insured people $2,000,000 plus the costs and profit for the company. This is a very simple example, but all insurance premiums are based on the probability or odds of something happening.

Adapted from: Hal B. Pickle and Royce L. Abrahamson, *Introduction to Business* (Santa Monica: Goodyear Publishing Co., 1980), p. 273. © Scott, Foresman and Company.

1. What is probability?
2. In your own words, explain how insurance premiums are calculated.

Questions for Discussion

1. Why do individuals, businesses, professional people, and even governments need liability insurance?
2. Do you think there should be a limit to the amount of money awarded in personal damage suits?
3. How would you assign a monetary value to human life?

chapter 4

Social Science

lesson
19

The Emancipation Proclamation

preview Preview this article by looking at the map. Why is the United Stated divided? What do you think caused the Civil War? Abraham Lincoln helped to end slavery with the Emancipation Proclamation. What does emancipate mean? What does proclaim mean? Read the article to find out how the Emancipation Proclamation helped the North win the Civil War.

The Emancipation Proclamation was a very important event in American history for two reasons. This proclamation helped to end slavery. It said that there should be no more slaves in the United States. It also helped to end the American Civil War, a terrible war between the North and the South.

The American Civil War began in 1861, when the southern states seceded from the United States. They made a new country, called the Confederate States of America (the Confederacy), because they did not want to be part of the United States anymore. On April 12, 1861, the Confederacy and the Union (the North) went to war.

The Civil War began because of political and economic reasons, but the most important reason for the war was slavery. Black slavery began in the United States in the 1600s when rich landowners brought Black people from Africa to the United States by force. The Black Africans worked as slaves on large farms, called plantations. They were not free; they were the property of the rich landowners. In the South, many people believed that slavery was necessary for the economy because slaves did a lot of work. The plantations could not exist without the slaves to work. However, many people believed that slavery was wrong. These people, called abolitionists, wanted to end, or abolish slavery.

In 1861, many people in the North believed that the war would be easy to win. There were more people, more railroads, more food, more factories, and more money in the North than in the South. Although the North had these advantages, the South won many battles in 1861 and 1862 because it had better generals. Also, the fighting in 1861 and 1862 occurred in the South. The Confederate soldiers had to fight to protect their homes.

By 1862 the North was losing many battles, and the abolitionists were not happy with President Lincoln because he was doing nothing to end slavery. These two things made the war unpopular. The people of the North were not happy about slavery or the war. President Lincoln wanted to do something to change the situation.

In 1862, Lincoln needed to win support for the war because the war was not popular in the North. He proclaimed that the southern states must return to the United States before January 1, 1863, or all slaves in the Confederacy would be declared "forever free." Lincoln made this proclamation five days after the U.S. Army won the battle of Antietam in September 1862.

The news of the Union victory at Antietam and the news of the proclamation pleased many people in the North. Of course, the South did not follow Lincoln's proclamation. The southern states did not return

to the United States, and on January 1, 1863, Lincoln issued the Emancipation Proclamation, which said that all slaves in the Confederacy were free. However, the Confederacy did not free the slaves.

The Emancipation Proclamation helped the North to win the war. After the Emancipation Proclamation, more Northerners supported the war. The war became more popular in the North. It also helped the North to win support of other countries. In fact, 1863 was the turning point of the war. The North began to win more battles. In July of 1863, the North won another important battle at Gettysburg. By 1865, the South could not continue the fight. The war ended in 1865 when the North won.

After the war, the U.S. government finished the work of the Emancipation Proclamation. The government passed a law. This law made slavery illegal, or against the law. Because the North won the war, the Confederacy became part of the United States again. Therefore, by law, the slaves were finally freed in 1865.

The Emancipation Proclamation is very important in American social history. President Lincoln's order is one of the country's most important acts of social equality. Also, it helped to end a terrible war.

Americans remember President Lincoln as the president who ended slavery. Many people believe that he was one of the best U. S. presidents. Unfortunately, one week after the end of the Civil War, President Lincoln was shot. He died the following day. The Emancipation Proclamation will always be one of his most significant acts.

708 words ________ time ________ wpm

MAIN IDEA

Choose the main idea for this article.

a. Abolitionists wanted to end slavery.

b. Lincoln was a great American president.

c. Slavery was very important to the economy of the South.

d. The Emancipation Proclamation is an important event.

COMPREHENSION QUESTIONS

Write **T** before true statements and **F** before false statements. Do not look back at the article.

______ 1. Slavery was the only cause of the American Civil War.

______ 2. Slavery in the United States began in 1860.

______ 3. It was easy for the North to win the war.

______ 4. The South won many battles in the first two years.

______ 5. In 1861 and 1862, the war was very popular in the North.

______ 6. Lincoln wanted the Emancipation Proclamation to win support for the war.

______ 7. The South did not free the slaves because of the Emancipation Proclamation.

______ 8. Gettysburg was an important Southern victory.

_______ 9. Lincoln died before the end of the War.

_______ 10. *In 1863, all slaves were really free because of the Emancipation Proclamation.

_______ number answered correctly

After correcting your answers, go back to the article to see why they are correct. Try to understand new words in context.

Write the line number of the sentence that states the main idea of the article. ________

Write the line numbers of the sentence or sentences that support your answer for question 10. ________

OUTLINE

To understand the main idea of the article, complete this outline.

I. The Emancipation Proclamation was important for two reasons.

A. ______________________________

B. ______________________________

II. There were two important events in 1861.

A. ______________________________

B. ______________________________

III. There were three major reasons for the Civil War.

A. ______________________________

B. ______________________________

C. ______________________________

IV. Both the North and the South had advantages.

A. The North had four advantages.

1. ______________________________

2. ______________________________

3. ______________________________

4. ______________________________

B. The South had two advantages.

1. ______________________________

2. ______________________________

V. Two things made the war unpopular in the North.

A. ______________________________

B. ______________________________

VI. Important events took place in two years of the war.

A. 1863:______________________________

B. 1865:______________________________

VII. There were two results of the war.

A. The new law______________________________

B. Lincoln______________________________

VIII. The importance of the Emancipation Proclamation

CAUSE AND EFFECT

Look at this example.

Southern plantation owners bought slaves because they needed workers.

cause = need for workers

effect = bought slaves

Events sometimes cause other events to happen. The *cause* is the reason for something. The *effect* is the result.

What are the effects of the following causes?

1. the secession of the southern states
2. the battle of Antietam
3. the South had better generals
4. the battle of Gettysburg
5. the preliminary proclamation of 1862
6. the Emancipation Proclamation

TIME LINE

A time line shows events in chronological order, in the order that they happened. Complete a time line for the events in the article.

1600s Slavery begins in U.S.

1861

SEQUENCE

These things happened before, after, and during the Civil War. Put them in order. Write 1, 2, 3, etc., in the spaces.

_______ The North won the battle of Antietam.

_______ The North won the war.

_______ The southern states seceded from the Union.

_______ President Lincoln made the Emancipation Proclamation.

_______ The slaves were really free.

_______ The Civil War began.

_______ The North was losing the war.

VOCABULARY IN CONTEXT

Read the following sentences. Choose the best meaning for the italicized word. Do not use your dictionary. Guess the meaning of the word from the context.

1. The southern states *seceded* from the Union. They did not want to be part of the United States anymore. They made a new country.
   a. became part of
   b. went away from, left
   c. came close to

2. They made a new country called the *Confederate States of America.*
   a. the northern states
   b. the Union
   c. a new country

3. Rich *landowners* brought Black people from Africa by force to work on their large farms.
   a. people who had a farm.
   b. Black people
   c. people from Africa

4. The Black Africans worked on large farms called *plantations.*
   a. Black Africans
   b. large farms
   c. landowners

5. The Black Africans were the property of the landowners. They were not free. They were *slaves.*
   a. free people
   b. landowners
   c. property

6. Without slaves to do the work, the plantation system could not *exist.*
   a. be
   b. continue
   c. both a and b

7. Many people believed that slavery was wrong. These people, called abolitionists, wanted to end or *abolish,* slavery.
   a. to finish
   b. to continue
   c. to believe

8. At first, the Northerners thought the war would be easy. But in 1861 and 1862 the South won many *battles.*
   a. wars
   b. fights in a war
   c. changes

9. In fact, 1863 was the *turning point* of the war. The North began to win more battles.
   a. when things began to change
   b. the beginning
   c. the end

SUBJECT-VERB IDENTIFICATION

Underline the simple subject and the simple verb in these sentences. Underline the subject one time and the verb two times.

1. On April 12, 1861, the Confederacy and the Union (the North) went to war.
2. The Civil War began because of political and economic reasons, but the most important reason for the war was slavery.
3. In the South, many people believed that slavery was necessary for the economy because slaves did a lot of work.
4. There were more people, more railroads, more food, more factories, and more money in the North then in the South.
5. Although the North had these advantages, the South won many battles in 1861 and 1862 because it had better generals.
6. By 1862 the North was losing many battles, and the abolitionists were not happy with President Lincoln because he was doing nothing to end slavery.
7. The news of the Union victory at Antietam and the news of the proclamation pleased many people in the North.
8. Of course, the South did not follow Lincoln's proclamation.
9. In fact, 1863 was the turning point of the war.
10. Unfortunately, one week after the end of the Civil War, President Lincoln was shot.

ROOTS AND AFFIXES

Read the sentences and look at the words. Divide the words into parts. Fill in the blanks or answer the questions. Try to discover the meaning of the roots and prefixes without your dictionary.

1. Lincoln was anti-slavery. He was not pro-slavery.
   (Hint: Lincoln was not pro-slavery; he was against it.)

   "pro" means ______________________.

   "anti" means ______________________.

2. If "claim" means to shout or to speak, what does "proclaim" mean?

   ____

3. Lincoln was not popular in the South. He was unpopular.
   It is against the law to rob banks. That is illegal.

   "il" and "un" mean ____________________.

4. Some countries import things. They carry things into the country. Some countries export things. Where do exported things go?

   ____

   Transport means to carry something across a distance. "Port" means

   ____________________.

5. "Sup" and "sub" are the same prefix. A submarine is a ship that sails under the sea. "Marine" means sea.

   "sub" or "sup" mean ____________________.

6. A bridge needs support to stand over the river.
   More people in the North supported the war after the Emancipation Proclamation.

   What does "support" mean? ____________________

7. Equal is an adjective. Everyone wants equal justice.
   Equality is important. The word "equality" is a noun.

   "ity" changes an adjective to a ____________________

Practice these roots and affixes. Read the sentences. Use your knowledge of roots and affixes to guess the meaning of the italicized word. Answer the questions.

1. Many people were *pro-Nixon* in 1972. Did these people support Nixon? ____________________
2. There were many *antiwar* protests during the Vietnam War. Did these people support the war? ____________________
3. The chair is *uncomfortable*. Would you like to sit in it for a long time? ____________________
4. The man is *illiterate*. Can he read? ____________________
5. The TV is *portable*. Can people carry it? ____________________
6. This car is *substandard*. Would you buy it? ____________________
7. An exponent is a little number above the line. A *subscript* is the opposite. Where do you write a subscript? ____________________

Study and learn these roots and affixes from the lesson.

pro	for
anti	against
un	not
il	not
port	carry
sub, sup	under
ity	noun suffix

READING GRAPHS

Look at Chapter 5, lesson 32, page 209 to learn how to read organizational charts.

lesson 20

Gandhi

preview To preview this article, look at the illustrations. Also, discuss with your classmates what you already know about Mahatma Gandhi. Read the article to learn more about his life.

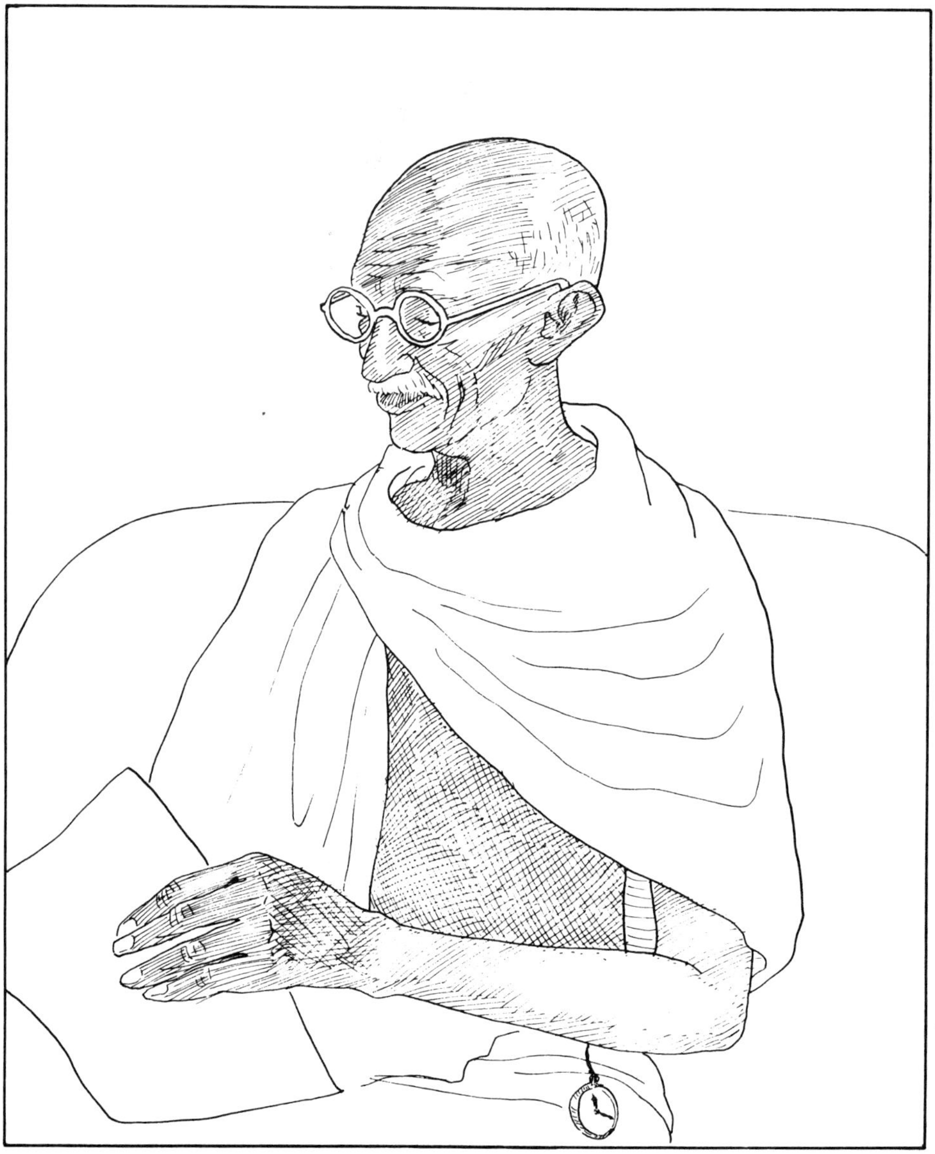

Mahatma Gandhi was one of the great leaders of the world. He wanted freedom and peace for all people. He helped to free India from British control.

His name was Mohandas Karamchand, but people called him Mahatma. This name means "great soul." Mohandas Karamchand was born on October 2, 1869 in Porbandar, India. He studied law in London, and in 1893 he began to practice law in South Africa.

In South Africa, Indians did not have the same rights as others. Gandhi did not like this racism. He believed that everyone should have the same rights. He worked for the Indian people in South Africa for twenty-one years. At one time, he organized a strike of Indian miners. The Indian mine workers did not go to work. Gandhi did not use violence. He fought with nonviolence, resistance, and strikes. The Indian word for nonviolent resistance is "satyagraha."

In 1915 Gandhi returned to India. He became the leader of the Indian Nationalist Movement, and he worked for the Independence of India. He wanted India to be free from Great Britain. Gandhi fought for freedom. He did not want India to be a British colony. He continued to use satyagraha, nonviolent means such as strikes and fasting. Fasting is when people do not eat.

During the fight for independence, Gandhi did many things. For example, he began a national program for spinning and weaving. The Indian people used to wear a long white cloth. The cloth was made of cotton. The Indian people grew the cotton, but then they sent it to England. Factories in England made cloth from the Indian cotton and sent it back to India. The people had to buy the British cloth in India. Gandhi wanted to make the cloth in India. Then it would not be as expensive as the British cloth, and more Indians would have jobs. It would help India have economic, social, and political freedom.

Gandhi's nonviolent fight for independence ended when Britain gave India her independence in 1947. However, after independence, different religious groups fought for power. The two major religions in India were the Muslims and the Hindus. Each group wanted to control the power in the new government. The two groups fought for that power. Gandhi tried to stop the fighting by fasting. He did not eat until the two groups agreed to stop fighting. He was successful in two large cities, Calcutta and Delhi, in 1947 and 1948. On January, 30, 1948, Gandhi was assassinated in New Delhi. He was shot when he was on the way to a prayer meeting.

Gandhi died for peace, and the whole world respects him for his peaceful ways of getting independence for his country.

451 words ________ time ________ wpm

MAIN IDEA

Choose the main idea for this article. All of the statements may be true, but one is the most important idea.

a. Gandhi fought without violence for peace, freedom, and equality.

b. Gandhi began his law practice in South Africa.

c. Gandhi helped India get her independence in 1947.

d. Gandhi died for peace.

COMPREHENSION QUESTIONS

Write **T** before true statements. Write **F** before false statements. Do not look at the article.

______ 1. Mahatma was Gandhi's real name.

______ 2. Gandhi was a young lawyer when he went to South Africa.

______ 3. Indians did not have the same freedoms as others in South Africa.

______ 4. Gandhi began to use nonviolent protest in South Africa.

______ 5. To refuse to eat is to fast.

______ 6. Gandhi wanted India to buy cloth from Great Britain.

______ 7. India did not grow cotton.

______ 8. Fasting was never successful for Gandhi.

______ 9. Gandhi wanted the Muslims and Hindus to live together in peace.

______ 10. *Before independence, Britain controlled India's economy.

______ number answered correctly

After correcting your answers, go back to the article and try to understand why they are correct. Try to understand the vocabulary in context.

Write the line number of the sentence that states the main idea of this article. ________

Write the line numbers of the sentence or sentences that support your answer to question 10. ________

VOCABULARY IN CONTEXT

Reread the text. Find these words. Write a definition from the text. The line number is in parenthesis.

1. racism (9) ______________________
2. strike (11) ______________________
3. satyagraha (14) ______________________
4. fasting (19) ______________________
5. assassinate (38) ______________________

SEQUENCE

These things happened in Gandhi's life. Put them in the order that they happened. Number them 1, 2, 3, and so on.

______ fast in jail to make Britain change her policy

______ return to India

______ assassination

______ study law

______ lead strikes in South Africa

______ try to stop Hindu-Muslim fights

______ begin a national program of spinning

______ independence for India

CLOZE

Read this paragraph from the article. Fill in the spaces with any word that completes the meaning. Use vocabulary and grammar clues to help you fill the spaces. Do not look at the article.

During the fight for independence, Gandhi did many things. __________ example, he began a __________ program for spinning and __________. The Indian people used __________ wear a long white __________. The cloth was made __________ cotton. The Indian people __________ the cotton, but they __________ it to England. Factories __________ England made cloth from __________ Indian cotton and sent ____ back to India. The ________ had to buy the ________ cloth in India. Gandhi ________ to make the cloth __________ India. Then it would __________ be as expensive as __________ British cloth, and more __________ would have jobs. It would help India to have economic, social, and political freedom from England.

WORD FORMS

It is important to know the different forms of words. That is, many words have one or more noun forms, a verb form, an adjective form, and perhaps an adverb form. To fill in each blank below, first decide what kind of word is necessary: noun, verb, or adjective. Second, find the correct word from the list and write the answer in the blank. Use a word from family 1 in sentence 1, a word from family 2 in sentence 2, and so on.

Verb	*Noun*	*Adjective*
1.	necessity	necessary
2. proclaim	proclamation	
3. abolish	abolition	
	abolitionist	
4.	politician	political
	politics	
5. free	freedom	free
6.	law	lawful
	lawyer	legal
		illegal

Verb	*Noun*	*Adjective*
7. resist	resistance	
8.	independence	independent
9.	expense	expensive
10.	violence	violent
11. succeed	success	successful

1. It is *necessary* to study before a test. A dictionary is a ____________ book. Everyone knows the ____________ of reading.
2. The boss ____________ a holiday.
   The boss's ____________ is popular with the employees.
3. Doctors try to ____________ disease.
   The ____________ of disease is important to doctors.
4. Many people like to discuss ____________ news.
   Many people like to discuss ____________.
   A ____________ is a person who tries to win an election.
5. Slaves are not ____________.
   The Civil War gave slaves their ____________.
6. Three years are necessary to study ____________.
   A ____________ is a person.
7. The ____________ of electricity produces heat and light.
   The chocolate cake looked delicious. It was difficult to ____________.
8. July 4 is the anniversary of America's ____________.
   In 1776, the United States became ____________ from England.
9. This apartment is very ____________.
   I cannot pay this ____________.
10. A tornado is a very ____________ storm. It causes much damage.
11. The ____________ completion of college made John happy.
    John ____________ in all of his courses.
    John's ____________ made his parents happy.

ADDITIONAL READING

Read this paragraph about Tolstoy and Gandhi. Then do the exercises below.

Tolstoy

Leo Tolstoy was a famous Russian writer of the nineteenth century. He lived between 1828 and 1910. He wrote many novels. Two of his most famous works are *War and Peace* and *Anna Karenina.* Tolstoy was born into a wealthy family. However, he was not happy that others were poor. He did not like living the rich life when others did not have food or money. In fact, Tolstoy often dressed like a peasant. He wanted the simple life.

In his novels, Tolstoy wrote about many things, but one of his most important themes was nonviolence. His ideas about nonviolence influenced two other famous leaders: Mahatma Gandhi and Martin Luther King. In fact, Tolstoy and Gandhi wrote letters to each other when Gandhi was in South Africa. Tolstoy's ideas helped Gandhi to use nonviolence.

Martin Luther King, the American civil rights leader, also believed in nonviolence. In his demonstrations during the 1960s, he always avoided violence. He helped to win more rights for Blacks.

Thus, Tolstoy the great Russian writer of the nineteenth century, greatly influenced two other great leaders of the peace movement.

1. If you are familiar with any of Tolstoy's works, share them with the class.
2. Find an encyclopedia. Read more information about Tolstoy, Gandhi, or Martin Luther King. Report your findings to your class.
3. In your own words, why do you think Gandhi, King, and Tolstoy believed in nonviolence?

Questions for Discussion

1. The North won the Civil War. Would life be different today if the South had won? If so, in what ways?
2. The Civil War had three causes: political, economic, and social. The social cause was slavery. See if you can find more information on the political and economic causes. Discuss your findings with the class.

3. Gandhi and others used nonviolence to bring about change. Is this the best way? Why or why not? Why do you think Gandhi preferred nonviolence?
4. Can you think of other leaders like Gandhi?

READING MAPS

To practice reading maps, turn to Chapter 5, lesson 33, on page 212.

lesson 21

Introduction to Linguistics

Preview Some people learn languages. Other people learn *about* languages. These people are linguists. The science is linguistics. To preview this lesson, discuss as many ideas about language and communication as possible.

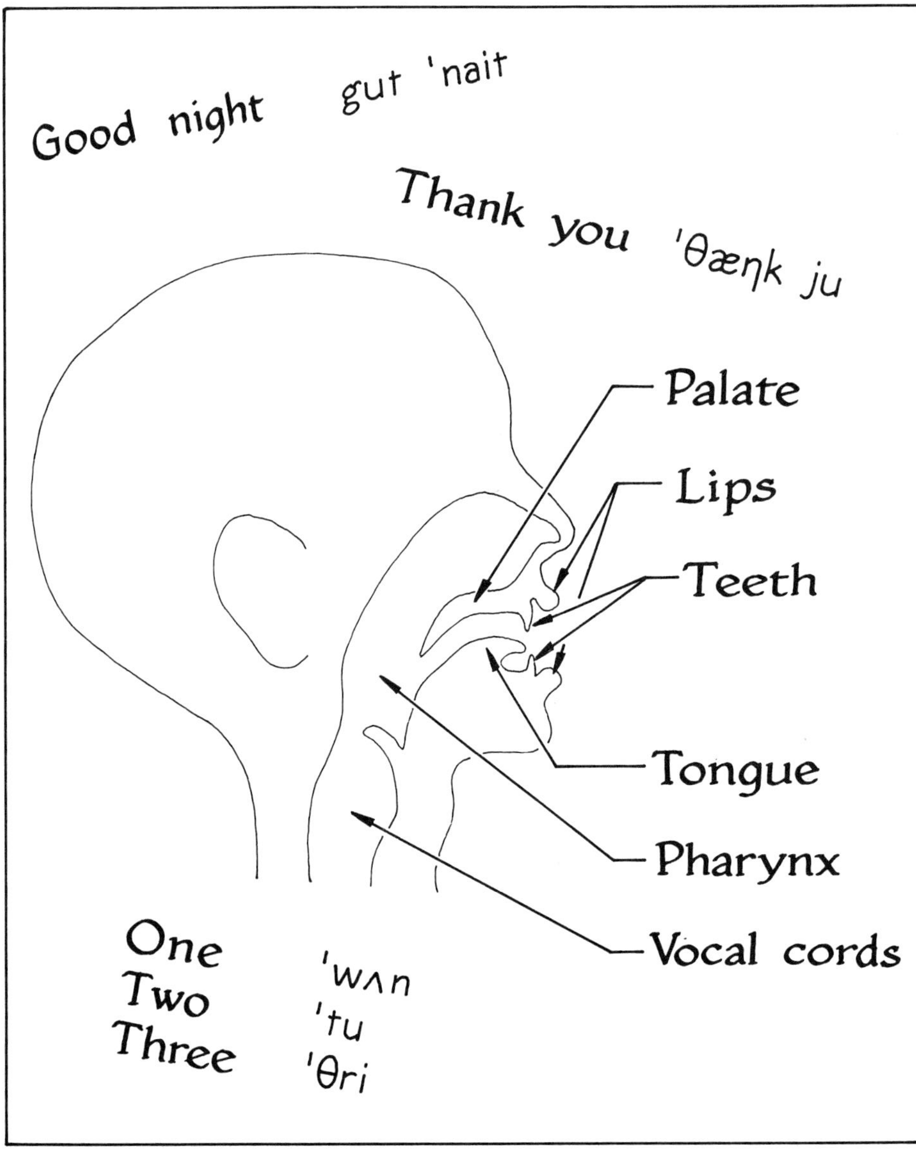

The study of linguistics is a new area of study in the twentieth century. Linguistics is the scientific study of language. Philosophers and linguists have studied languages for many centuries, but the modern science of linguistics became popular in the United States in the nineteenth and twentieth centuries. The work of the linguist is to describe language and communication. Also, a linguist provides information for people who learn or teach languages. There are many different parts of the study of linguistics: historical linguistics, sociolinguistics, psycholinguistics, and descriptive linguistics, which includes phonology, (the study of sounds), and syntax.

Historical linguistics is a very interesting area of linguistics. In this area, people study the old forms of languages. For example, Old English is impossible for most people to read today. English has changed very much since the fifth century.

Another kind of linguist studies sociolinguistics. This kind of linguist studies language in society. For example, a sociolinguist studies language differences between women and men, or between young and old, in formal and informal situations.

Psycholinguistics is the study of language and the mind. Some scientists are very interested in first-language learning. How do children learn a first language? How do people learn to read? How do people learn grammar? These are questions that a psycholinguist would ask.

Many linguists study other areas of linguistics. One of these areas is the study of sounds. The study of sounds is *phonology*. A phonologist is a linguist who studies the sounds of language. This linguist studies the way people make sounds. To make a sound of a language, people use their lips, teeth, tongue, palate, glottis, pharynx, and several other parts of the mouth and throat. Scientists describe sounds by where and how they are made. Phonologists also use a special alphabet to write these sounds. In this phonetic alphabet, each symbol represents one sound. In the English alphabet, this is not true. In English, the letter *o*, for example, has many different sounds as in pot, come, women, and boat. Phonologists use a different symbol for each sound.

pot	pɑt
come	kʌm
women	wɪmən
boat	bówt

Some sounds are voiced and some sounds are voiceless. A *voiced* sound happens when the vocal chords in the throat vibrate, or move back and forth. For a *voiceless* sound, the vocal chords are relaxed and do not move. For example, the beginning sound in "see" is voiceless. The beginning sound in "zoo" is voiced. It is easy to hear and feel voicing. To feel voicing, place your fingers on the throat and say "zee," then say "ess." The buzzing sound with the *z* is voicing. This is an example of only one part of phonology.

Linguists who study sounds of language are very important. These scientists find information for people who are learning or teaching a language. These linguists can find differences between the sounds of languages. With this information they can help people learn a second language better.

There are many other kinds of linguists. Other linguists study words. It is important to know how words come into a language. Many English words come from Latin, Greek, or German, but new words are always entering a language. The word "radar" entered English in the middle of the twentieth century. It comes from *ra*dio *d*etecting *a*nd *r*anging. There are many other examples: scuba, microwaveable, microprocessor, and robotics.

Other linguists study sentences. This area is called syntax. Syntax is the group of rules for putting words in order. Words cannot be used in any order. There are rules in every language. Linguists try to discover these rules.

Linguistics is a new science. It has many branches or parts. There are many different areas a student can study in linguistics. It is certainly one of the exciting fields of the twentieth century.

633 words ________ time ________ wpm

MAIN IDEA

Choose the main idea for this article.

a. Historical linguists study old languages.

b. Linguistics is a new area of study, and there are many parts to it.

c. Phonologists use a special alphabet to write language.

d. Every language has grammar rules and special sounds.

Linguists study many different things. Circle the things that they study. *Do not* look back at the reading.

1. history
2. history of language
3. the differences between men and women
4. how young people and old people speak
5. how children learn language
6. how children learn to read
7. how to speak Chinese
8. how sounds are made
9. the words and grammar of languages

COMPREHENSION QUESTIONS

Write **T** before true statements. Write **F** before false statements. *Do not* look back at the reading.

_______ 1. Linguistics is the scientific study of language.

_______ 2. Linguists can help people to teach and learn languages.

_______ 3. Sociolinguists study old forms of languages.

_______ 4. A phonologist is a linguist who studies sounds.

_______ 5. In the English alphabet, each letter has only one sound.

_______ 6. Voicing is a part of phonology.

_______ 7. Linguists do not study word order or grammar rules.

_______ 8. *A linguist is a person who learns to speak many languages.

_______ 9. *Languages change over many years.

_______ 10. *Linguists know exactly how people learn their first language.

_______ number answered correctly

After you correct your answers, go back to the article and see why the answers are correct. Try to guess the meaning of new words from the context.

Write the line number of the sentence that states the main idea of this article. ________

Write the line numbers of the sentence or sentences that support your answers to questions 8 ________, 9 ________, and 10 ________.

VOCABULARY IN CONTEXT

Find these words in the article. The line numbers are in parentheses. Write a definition from the text.

1. informal (18) ________________________________
2. symbol (30) ________________________________
3. vibrate (39) ________________________________
4. relaxed (40) ________________________________
5. branch (62) ________________________________

SUBJECT-VERB IDENTIFICATION

Underline the subject and verb in these sentences. Underline the subject one time and the verb two times.

1. The work of the linguist is to describe language and communication.
2. For example, Old English is impossible for most people to read today.
3. How do children learn a first language?
4. A phonologist is a linguist who studies the sounds of language.
5. This linguist studies the way people make sounds.
6. In the English alphabet, this is not true.
7. Some sounds are voiced, and some sounds are voiceless.
8. For a voiceless sound, the vocal chords are relaxed and do not move.
9. Linguists who study sounds of language are very important.
10. It is important to know how words come into a language.

ROOTS AND AFFIXES

Read the sentences. Pay attention to the roots and affixes in the words. Try to guess the meaning of the parts of the words.

1. Linguistics is the study of languages.
   A linguist studies languages.
   A bilingual person speaks two languages.

   "ling" means ________________.

2. "Social" is the adjective from "society."
   A society is a group of people who live together.
   "Social" means "to like to be together with people."
   Sociology is the study of people.

   "soci" means ________________.

3. A psychologist studies the human mind.
   Psychology is the study of the mind.
   A psychosomatic illness is in the mind.
   Psycholinguistics is the study of language and the mind.

   "psych" means ________________.

4. A phonologist studies the sounds of a language.
   A telephone is a tool that lets you speak over long distances.
   A phonograph is a stereo or record player.

   "phon" means ________________.

5. A voiceless sound has no voicing.
   A penniless person has no money.
   A fearless person has no fear.

   "less" means ________________.

Study and learn these roots and affixes from this lesson.

ling	language
soci	people
psycho	mind
phon	sound
less	without

PRONOUN REFERENCE

Pronouns usually replace nouns, but *it* is sometimes the subject of an indefinite sentence. In this case, it does not replace any noun. Read these sentences from the text. A word is italicized. Circle the noun that it refers to. If *it* is indefinite, write *I*.

1. Historical linguistics is a very interesting area of linguistics. In *this* area, people study the old forms of languages.
2. Another kind of linguist studies sociolinguistics. *This kind* of linguist studies language and society.
3. How do children learn a first language? How do people learn to read? How do people learn grammar? *These* are questions that a psycholinguist would ask.
4. Phonologists also use a special alphabet to write these sounds. In *this* alphabet, each symbol represents one sound.
5. *It* is easy to hear voicing.
6. Linguists who study sounds of language are very important. These scientists find information for people who are learning or teaching a language. *These* linguists can find differences between the sound of languages. With *this* information *they* can help people learn a second language better.
7. Linguistics is a new science. *It* has many branches or parts.

PASSIVE

Many sentences use passive verbs. Read these sentences from the article carefully. Then underline the complete passive verb and identify the doer.

1. Scientists describe sounds by where and how they are made.
2. For a voiceless sound, the vocal chords are relaxed and do not move.
3. Words cannot be used in any order.

lesson
22

Comparative Linguistics

preview What differences are there between your language and English? What similarities are there? Do these things make English easy or difficult to learn?

They did the homework yesterday.

Sie haben die Hausarbeit gestern gemacht.

They the homework yesterday did

Ils ont fini les devoirs hier.

They did (finished) the homework yesterday

أمس الواجب عملوا

ams al waajib a'malou

Yesterday the homework they did

昨日 彼ら は その 宿題 を しました.

Sakujitsu karera wa sono shukudai o shimashita.

Yesterday they (subject or topic marker) the homework (object particle) did

Ellos hicieron la tarea ayer.

They did the homework yesterday.

One job of linguists is to help people learn languages. Sometimes, linguists look at two languages to find similarities and differences. This information often helps teachers and students of second languages. Although many linguists work in other areas today, it is still important for students to examine these differences. Knowing about these things can help students understand languages better. Linguists examine several areas as part of a comparative study: sounds, vocabulary, and grammar.

One area of contrast in many languages is the sounds of a language. Languages have different sounds. For example the *l* sound (as in *l*ife) and the *r* sound (as in *r*ound) are different in English. In other words, changing an *l* to an *r* makes a difference in meaning. For example, *river* and *liver* are two different words in English. In Japanese, and other languages, this difference does not exist. In Japanese, these two sounds mean the same thing. They are only variations of the same sound. Therefore, when a speaker of Japanese learns English, teachers can expect errors in pronouncing *l* and *r*. Another example is with Spanish *b* and *v*. In English, these sounds make a difference in meaning; in Spanish they do not. Other languages have many sounds that are difficult for a speaker of English to hear and produce. For example, the first sound of Khalid, an Arabic name, is not in English. An English speaker would make a *k* sound (as in *k*itten). This would be an error.

Another area of contrast is vocabulary. Because a lot of English vocabulary comes from Latin and French, many speakers of French, Italian, and Spanish believe that vocabulary is easy in English. This is not always true. It is true that many words are the same. However, there are some words called false cognates. A false cognate looks like a word in the native language, but it has a different meaning in the second language. For example, the English word "actually" (in truth) and the French word "actuellement" (now) seem the same, but they have different meanings.

An additional area of contrast is grammar. Very often students try to write a second language in their native grammar. Therefore, an Arabic-speaking student may say, "The book which I bought *it* this morning. . . ." This sentence has a double object, *which* and *it*. This is correct in Arabic, but not in English. In English, we say, "The book which I bought this morning. . . ." A Spanish speaker may write, "Lives many people in this city." This sentence is correct word order for Spanish, but not for English. First, the word people is plural in English. Second, the verb in English comes after the subject. In English, we would write, "Many people live in this city." A final example comes from Japanese. In Japanese, articles (a, an, the) are not expressed. The idea of articles is part of Japanese, but in Japanese, articles are expressed in a different way. It is not surprising for Japanese speakers to make errors with articles in English.

Linguists can study language. Some linguists compare languages. They look at the similarities and differences. They use this information to predict errors that students may make if they learn a second language. This information helps both teachers and students.

545 words ________ time ________ wpm

MAIN IDEA

Choose the main idea for this article.

a. The Japanese *l* and *r* are different from the English *l* and *r*.

b. It is easy to learn English vocabulary if you know French vocabulary.

c. A study of grammar can show possible errors in second language learning.

d. Linguists sometimes study sounds, vocabulary, and grammar to find similarities and differences between languages.

COMPREHENSION QUESTIONS

Write **T** before true statements. Write **F** before false statements. *Do not* look back at the article.

______ 1. Linguists cannot help people learn language.

______ 2. Differences are things that are not the same.

______ 3. Some languages have different sounds from other languages.

______ 4. *English, Japanese, Spanish, and Arabic all have exactly the same sounds.

______ 5. False cognates make it difficult to learn a language.

______ 6. Students should write the second language with first-language grammar.

______ 7. Differences between languages may exist in sounds and vocabulary but not in grammar.

______ 8. *Cognates are two similar words in two different languages that mean the same thing.

______ 9. *Languages that are similar may be different in important ways.

_______ 10. *Language students make errors where their languages are different from English.

_______ number answered correctly

After correcting your answers, go back to the article to see why they are correct. Try to discover the meaning of new words from the context.

Write the line number of the sentence that states the main idea of this article. _________

Write the line numbers of the sentence or sentences that support your answer from questions 8 _________, 9 _________, and 10 _________.

VOCABULARY IN CONTEXT

Find the words in the article. The line number is in parentheses. Write a definition from the text.

1. similarities (2) ______________________________
2. contrast (8) ______________________________
3. errors (16) ______________________________
4. false cognates (26) ______________________________
5. compare (44) ______________________________

WORD FORMS

It is important to know the different forms of words. That is, many words have one or more noun forms, a verb form, an adjective form, and perhaps an adverb form. To fill in each blank below, first decide what kind of word is necessary: noun, verb, or adjective. Second, find the correct word from the list and write the answer in the blank. Use a word from family 1 in sentence 1, a word from family 2 in sentence 2, and so on.

Verb	*Noun*	*Adjective*
1.	science scientist	scientific
2.	possibility	impossible possible

Verb	*Noun*	*Adjective*
3. socialize	society sociologist sociology	social
4.	importance	important
5. informed	information	informative
6. discover	discovery	
7. examine	examination	
8. compare	comparison	comparative
9. differ	difference	different
10. predict	prediction	predictable

1. A person who studies something about science is a *scientist*. Many people have made ____________ discoveries in the twentieth century. ____________ is very interesting.

2. The ____________ of rain made the people cancel the picnic.
   If something can happen, it is ____________.
   If something cannot happen, it is ____________.

3. A person who studies sociology is a ____________.
   Human beings are ____________.
   Many people like to ____________ with other people.

4. Reading is an ____________ skill.
   The ____________ of reading for a college student is great.

5. At the university, students must go to the library to find ____________.
   Mary ____________ me yesterday that she would be out of town next week.

6. The ____________ of the atom was a milestone in scientific history.
   Human beings will ____________ many more things in the future.

7. You must ____________ these sentences very carefully.
   The ____________ of these sentences will help you find the answer.

8. A ____________ of New York and Paris shows many contrasts.

   Before you buy a car, ____________ the price with those of other dealers.

   ____________ buying can save you money.

9. What is the ____________ of 4 minus 2?

   Mary and John do not agree. They ____________ on that matter.

10. In the desert, the ____________ weather is hot and sunny.

    It is very difficult to ____________ the weather.

    Every night, the meteorologist gives a ____________ about the next day's weather.

CLOZE

Fill in the blanks with any word that completes the meaning. Read the paragraph carefully before you begin. Use vocabulary and grammar clues to help you decide on the words. Do not look back at the articles.

One area of contrast in many languages is sounds of a language. Languages have ____________ sounds. For example the *l* ____________ (as in *l*ife) and ____________ *r* sound (as in ____________) are different in English. ____________ other words, changing an ____________ to an *r* makes ____________ difference in meaning. For ____________, *river* and *liver* are ____________ different words in English. ____________ Japanese and other languages, ____________ difference does not exist. ____________ Japanese, these two sounds ____________ the same thing. They ____________ only variations of the ____________ sound. Therefore, when a ____________ of Japanese learns English, ____________ can expect errors in ____________ *l* and *r*. Another ____________ is with Spanish *b* ____________ *v*. In English, these ____________ are different; in Spanish ____________ are not. Other languages ____________ many sounds that are ____________ for a speaker of ____________ to hear and produce. ____________ example, the first sound ____________ Khalid, an Arabic name, ____________ not in English. An ____________ speaker makes a *k* ____________ (as in *k*itten). This is an error.

ADDITIONAL READING

Read this article about dialects. Answer the questions that follow.

Dialects

Languages have dialects. A dialect is a variation of a language. This means that there are differences within a language. For example, French is spoken in Paris. There is a slightly different French in Canada. The French spoken in Africa is different still. However, speakers of these three dialects can understand each other. Usually, a dialect is a variety of a language that other speakers of the language can understand; dialects are usually mutually intelligible.

Not all dialects of Chinese are mutually intelligible. Chinese has many dialects. Speakers of Mandarin Chinese and Cantonese Chinese cannot communicate with each other in the spoken language. To communicate, they must write to each other or use a second language. Still, these two Chinese languages are dialects because China is one country and one culture with one language.

The differences between American English and British English are not as great as the differences in Chinese dialects. Two of the differences between American and British English are vocabulary and spelling. In American English we say elevator, truck, and apartment. The British say lift, lorry, and flat. Another difference is spelling. In American English we write honor, meter, and realize. In British English, these words are honour, metre, and realise.

Dialects are an interesting part of language study. All languages have dialects. Usually speakers of one dialect can understand speakers of another dialect.

1. In your own words, what is a dialect of a language?
2. How would a British speaker write the word color? theater?
3. Explain what is meant by the phrase "mutually intelligible."

Questions for Discussion

1. Discuss the dialects of your language.
2. Do you think it is easier to learn a second language that is similar to your native language, or is it easier to learn a second language that is completely different?
3. Can you give examples of vocabulary from your language that show how words are borrowed? Are there any words from your language in English?
4. What are the most difficult sounds for you to make in English? What are the easiest?
5. If English is your third language, does your second language help you to learn your third language?
6. What is the most difficult thing about learning a language?

lesson
23

History of the English Language

Preview Preview this article by thinking about how languages change. Do you know anything about the history of your language?

Old English - Opening lines of *Beowulf*

Hwæt! We Gar-Dena in gear-dagum
peod-cyninga, prym gefrunon,
hu ða æpelingas ellen fremedon!
Oft Scyld Scefing sceapena preatum
monegum maegpum meodo-setla
ofteah

Middle English - Opening lines of *The Tales of Canterbury*
by Geoffrey Chaucer

Whan that April with his shoures soote
The droghte of March hath perced to the roote,
And bathed every veyne in swich licour
Of which vertu engendred is the flour;
Whan Zephirus eek with his sweete breeth

The history of the English language is well known to scholars. Linguists who study it are fortunate because there are many written records to help them. The history of English began 5,000 or 6,000 thousand years ago and continues to the present time.

English is a part of a group of languages called Indo-European. There are many Indo-European languages today. There is, for example, the Italic group. This group includes Latin and all Latin languages (French, Spanish, Italian, and others). There is also the Slavic group. This group includes Russian, Polish, and Czech. Urdu is a member of the Indic group, and Latvian is a member of the Baltic group. English is a member of the Germanic group. German, Dutch, and Swedish are also members of the Germanic group. There are other groups, too.

Germanic people brought English to England in the fifth century A.D. Before this time, the Romans, who spoke Latin, were living in England and in western Europe. When the Roman Empire lost power, four Germanic groups from western Europe (the Saxons, the Angles, the Frisians, and the Jutes) were able to conquer England. The Celts, who were already living in England, moved to the north of England.

This period of time, the fifth century A.D., is the beginning of the time when Old English was used. Old English is similar to modern German. This means that Old English has many endings for words. These endings are for nouns, verbs, and adjectives. Because of the endings, the order of words was not very important in Old English. Also, spelling, pronunciation, and vocabulary were very different in Old English. There were few Latin or French words in English at that time. Today, there are many Latin and French words in English.

The Middle English period is from the eleventh century to the fifteenth century. One event during this time caused great changes in English vocabulary. In A.D. 1066, England was conquered by the Normans from France. Their leader was William the Conqueror, and they spoke French. During this period, from 1066 to approximately 1200, the upper classes in England spoke French. Most other people still spoke English, but many people were bilingual, speaking both French and English. Beginning at this time, many Germanic words were lost. French words took their place. French words appeared in many areas such as in government, law, warfare, art, medicine. Some examples of words that came from French during this time are parliament, empire, justice, crime, combat, sculpture, beauty, and surgeon. There are many more examples.

There are many vocabulary changes during the Middle English period, but there were more changes in grammar. Many of the word endings of Old English were lost, and word order became more important. There were many more grammatical changes than vocabulary changes during the Middle English period.

The Modern English period began around the fifteenth century. Today we are still in the Modern English period. In this period, vocabulary is changing rapidly; grammar is changing slowly. At the beginning of this period, the printing press, education, and better communication helped English vocabulary to change. Today, it is interesting to look at words in a science lesson, for example. Many science words did not exist several years ago. Words from the computer industry are also examples: microprocessor, chip, bit, byte.

English has had a very long and varied history. It began in the fifth century and continues to the present. It has passed through three periods: Old, Middle, and Modern English. Today's English has different vocabulary, grammar, pronunciation, and spelling from Old English. English is related to German, but much of its vocabulary comes from French and Latin.

611 words ________ time ________ wpm

MAIN IDEA

Choose the main idea for this article.

a. The English language is 5,000 or 6,000 years old and has gone through three separate periods.

b. The English language is an Indo-European language.

b. Many European languages belong to the Indo-European family.

d. The Norman invasion of 1066 caused a great change in the vocabulary of English.

Circle the three languages that have influenced English the most.

Urdu

Latin

French

Russian

German

Arabic

Polish

COMPREHENSION QUESTIONS

______ 1. *Early English speakers probably wrote many things.

______ 2. The history of English is 10,000 years old.

______ 3. *Russian, German, French, Latvian, and English may all have come from the same language—Indo-European.

______ 4. *The fall of Rome permitted Germanic people to conquer England.

______ 5. Modern English is like modern German.

______ 6. Word order is not very important in modern English.

______ 7. There were many grammatical changes during the middle English period.

______ 8. After the Norman conquest, people in England stopped speaking English.

______ 9. The English language is not changing today.

______ 10. Modern English vocabulary and grammar are different from Old English.

______ number answered correctly

After correcting your answers, go back to the reading to find out why your answers are correct. Try to discover the meaning of new words from the context.

Write the line number of the sentence that states the main idea of this article. ________

Write the line numbers of the sentence or sentences that support your answer to questions 1 ________, 3 ________, and 4 ________.

SEQUENCE

Putting ideas in order is a very important reading skill. Arrange the list of events in English history in order. Write the numbers 1, 2, 3, and so on. If necessary, go back to the article and check which events happened before others.

______ Many French words came into English.

______ Germanic people came to England

_______ The Normans conquered England.

_______ The Celts moved to northern England.

_______ The Modern English period began.

_______ English had many word endings.

_______ The Roman Empire fell.

VOCABULARY IN CONTEXT

Find the words in the article. The line numbers are in parantheses. Write a definition from the text.

1. scholars (1) ______________________________
2. include (7) ______________________________
3. modern (45) ______________________________
4. endings (21) ______________________________
5. bilingual (33) ______________________________
6. appear (35) ______________________________
7. rapidly (47) ______________________________

ROOTS AND AFFIXES

Read the problems. Try to discover the meaning of new suffixes and roots.

1. If a boss does not hire someone because of his or her race then this is *racism.*
   If a boss does not hire someone because of his or her sex, then this is *sexism.*
   If someone likes material things, then this is *materialism.* Other examples are *capitalism, Marxism,* and *socialism.*

   "ism" means ____________________.

2. A *miner* is one who mines.
   A *leader* is one who leads.
   A *can opener* is something to open a can.

   "er" means ____________________.

3. A *factory* is a place where people make things.
To *manufacture* used to mean "to make by hand."

"fact" means ______________________.

4. In Japanese, the "l" sound and the "r" sound are *variations* of the same sound. In English these sounds are different. American English and British English are *variations* of the same language.
English has had a long, *varied* history.

"vari" means ______________________.

5. John and Mary have *similar* tastes. They both like fish.
Betty and John are not *similar* in any way. He likes hot, spicy food; she likes mild foods.
Bob and Tom are *similar* in appearance. Both are tall, with dark hair and glasses.
English and French have a *similar* vocabulary. English and Japanese do not.

"simil" means ______________________.

Study and learn these roots and affixes.

ism	makes a noun
er	the person who
fact	to make
vari	to be different
simil	to be the same

PRONOUN REFERENCE

Read these sentences from the article. The pronoun is italicized. Circle the noun to which the pronoun refers.

1. Linguists who study the history of English are fortunate because there are many written records to help *them*.
2. Germanic people brought English to England in the fifth century A.D. Before *this time*, the Romans lived in England.
3. In A.D. 1066, England was conquered by the Normans from France. *Their* leader was William the Conqueror, and *they* spoke French.

4. Beginning at this time, many Germanic words were lost. French words took *their* place.
5. Today, *it* is interesting to look at words in a science lesson, for example.

SUBJECT-VERB IDENTIFICATION

Underline the subject one time. Underline the verb two times.

1. Linguists who study the history of English are fortunate because there are many written records to help them.
2. The history of English began 5,000 or 6,000 years ago and continues to the present time.
3. Before this time, the Romans, who spoke Latin, were living in England and in Western Europe.
4. When the Roman Empire lost power, four Germanic groups from western Europe (the Saxons, the Angles, the Frisians, and the Jutes) were able to conquer England.
5. Also, spelling, pronunciation, and vocabulary were very different in Old English.
6. In A.D. 1066, England was conquered by the Normans from France.
7. Beginning at this time, many Germanic words were lost.

lesson
24

Cognitive versus Behavioral Learning

preview To preview this article, look at the title and the illustrations. How do animals and humans learn? What do we know about the human mind?

Scientists always try to understand new things. Some things are very difficult to understand, so scientists make theories to describe them. A *theory* is an explanation of things that a scientist sees. Albert Einstein, for example, made theories about physics. Scientists also make theories about biology, chemistry, and many other subjects. Psychologists study how people use their minds, and they make theories about how people learn. There are two kinds of learning theories: behavioral and cognitive.

Behavioral learning theories were very popular in the first part of the twentieth century. In behavioral theories, an important word is "observable." Behaviorists *observe* or *see* things. They do not discuss things that happen in the mind—the mental processes—because they cannot see what happens inside the brain. Behaviorists believe that scientists cannot discuss mental processes because they cannot see them.

Behaviorists can often see two things: a stimulus and a response. A *stimulus* is anything that causes an action. A *response* is anything someone does because of a stimulus. For example, a loud sound will make people jump. The stimulus is a loud noise. The response is jumping. Behaviorist theories are often called S-R theories (for stimulus-response).

One famous example of behavioral learning is *operant conditioning*. B.F. Skinner wrote about operant conditioning. In this kind of learning, behavior is learned because of a reward called reinforcement. A reinforcement is anything that helps certain behavior to happen again. For example, if someone gives food to a dog when the dog picks up a shoe, probably the dog will pick up the shoe again to get more food. Food is the reinforcement. Picking up the shoe is the response to the stimulus. In operant conditioning, someone gives reinforcement for behavior that is close to the desired, or wanted, behavior again and again. Finally, the desired behavior is reached. By this method, birds can learn to play games, dogs can learn tricks, and people can learn many things.

Operant conditioning explains some things about learning. But many psychologists believe that it does not explain enough about learning. It is a behavioral theory. Mental processes are not part of the theory. Stimulus, response, reinforcement, and observed behavior are important in behavioral theories.

Other theories of learning are cognitive theories. Cognitive psychologists believe that learning is very complex. For example, one psychologist, Ausubel, believes there is a cognitive structure. The cognitive structure includes all the things that a person knows. When people learn, new ideas become part of the cognitive structure. New ideas join to form more new ideas. These new ideas also become part of the cognitive structure. The cognitive structure helps people learn more new things.

Piaget is another very famous cognitive psychologist. His work discusses learning, growth, and mental (cognitive) structures. Piaget believes in schemata. A schema consists of both observable behavior and unobservable mental processes.

To summarize, behavioral psychologists look at stimulus, response, and reinforcement. They do not try to describe the mental process because they cannot see them. Cognitive psychologists believe that the unobservable mental processes are more important than the observable behaviors.

Of the two kinds of learning theories, behavioral and cognitive, many psychologists today seem to prefer cognitive theories. But it is very important to remember that no theory explains everything. A theory may not be the same as truth. As scientists and psychologists learn more, theories must change. Psychologists always make new theories. As psychologists learn more and more about the human brain and mind, new learning theories will develop.

582 words ________ time ________ wpm

MAIN IDEA

Choose the main idea for this article.

a. Behavioral learning can explain why animals learn tricks.

b. Scientists always make new theories.

c. Cognitive psychologists believe mental processes are very important.

d. There are two theories of learning: behavioral and cognitive.

COMPREHENSION QUESTIONS

Write **T** before true statements and **F** before false statements.

______ 1. A theory is the same as the truth.

______ 2. The word "observable" is important to the cognitive psychologists.

______ 3. *Psychologists are still learning things about the human brain.

______ 4. B.F. Skinner wrote about the importance of reinforcement in learning.

_______ 5. A reinforcement is something that helps a behavior to happen again.

_______ 6. All psychologists agree that behavioral theories are better than cognitive theories.

_______ 7. Piaget is a very famous behaviorist.

_______ 8. Cognitive psychologists believe that old ideas help people learn new things.

_______ 9. A stimulus is something that causes a behavior.

_______ 10. *Learning is not very complicated.

_______ number answered correctly

After correcting your answers, go back to the article to see why they are correct. Try to discover the meaning of the new words in context.

Write the line number of the sentence that states the main idea of this article. _________

Write the line numbers of the sentence or sentences that support your answer for questions 3 _________ and 10 _________.

VOCABULARY IN CONTEXT

Find the words in the article; the line number is in parentheses. Match the new word in the first column with its definition in the second column.

_______	1.	theory (3)	a. things that happen in the mind
_______	2.	observe (10)	b. what happens after a stimulus; an answer
_______	3.	mental process (11)	c. well known
_______	4.	response (15)	d. briefly; in conclusion
_______	5.	famous (19)	e. explanation of what a scientist sees
_______	6.	reward (21)	f. a reinforcement; a prize
_______	7.	to summarize (46)	g. see

SUBJECT-VERB IDENTIFICATION

Underline the subject and verb in these sentences. Underline the subject one time, and underline the verb two times.

1. Psychologists study how people use their minds, and they make theories about how people learn.
2. They do not discuss things that happen in the mind—the mental processesses—because they cannot see what happens inside the brain.
3. In this kind of learning, behavior is learned because of a reward called reinforcement.
4. For example, if someone gives food to a dog when the dog picks up a shoe, probably the dog will pick up the shoe again to get more food.
5. Picking up the shoe is the response to a stimulus.
6. Finally, the desired behavior is reached.
7. They do not try to describe the mental process because they cannot see them.
8. Of the two kinds of learning theories, behavioral and cognitive, many psychologists today seem to prefer cognitive theories.

WORD FORMS

Learn these different forms of words. Use a word from family 1 in sentence 1 below, a word from family 2 in sentence 2, and so on.

Noun	*Verb*	*Adjective*
1. existence	exist	
2. similarity		similar to
3. government	govern	
governor		
4. beginning	begins	
5. pronunciation	pronounce	
6. growth	grow	
7. psychologist		psychological
psychology		
8. response	respond	

Noun	*Verb*	*Adjective*
9. discussion	discuss	
10. explanation	explain	

1. The *existence* of some isotopes was not known until the twentieth century.
   It is not easy to ____________ in the desert.
2. An atom is ____________ an isotope in many ways.
   The ____________ of atoms and isotopes is great.
3. The ____________ of the United States is in Washington D.C.
   The United States has a president; it does not have a ____________.
   It is not easy to ____________ a country.
4. The ____________ of the lesson was very difficult.
   When someone ____________ something new, it is often difficult.
5. What is the correct ____________ of "often"?
   How do you ____________ that word?
6. Some plants ____________ quickly.
   It is easy to measure their ____________.
7. A ____________ is a person who studies ____________.
8. I sent them a letter, but they did not ____________.
   They did not send me a ____________.
9. Last night, we had a ____________ about television.
   We did not ____________ our favorite shows.
10. Please ____________ where the post office is.
    What is the ____________ about the accident?

ADDITIONAL READING

Read this article about Pavlov's experiments and answer the questions that follow.

Pavlov's Experiments

Another kind of behavioral theory of learning is classical conditioning. The most famous person in this area is Pavlov. Pavlov experimented with dogs. He noticed that dogs salivate as they eat. In other words, a liquid called saliva entered the dog's mouth when food is in the mouth. Pavlov experimented to see if dogs could learn to salivate in other situations. At the beginning of the experiment, Pavlov rang a bell when he fed the dogs. After some time, Pavlov rang the bell, but he did not feed the dogs. The dogs salivated at the sound of the bell even when there was no food. The dogs learned a new behavior. They learned to salivate in a new situation.

The work of Pavlov explains some kinds of learning. It does not explain all kinds. Many psychologists believe that classical conditioning does not explain more complicated kinds of learning.

1. In your own words, describe Pavlov's experiments.
2. What did scientists learn from Pavlov?
3. What do you think "conditioning" means in general?

CLOZE

Read this paragraph from the article. Do not look back at the article. Fill in the blanks with any word that completes the meaning. Use grammar and vocabulary clues to help you find the words.

Scientists always try to understand and explain new things. Some things ____________ very difficult to understand, ____________ scientists make theories to ____________ them. A theory is ____________ explanation of things that ____________ scientist sees. ____________ Einstein, for example, made theories ____________ physics. Scientists also make ____________ about biology, chemistry, and ____________ other subjects. Psychologists study ____________ people use their minds, and ____________ make theories about how ____________ learn. There are two kinds of learning theories: behavioral and cognitive theories.

READING TABLES

To learn how to read tables, turn to page 216, chapter 5, lesson 34.

lesson
25

Intelligence and IQ

preview What is intelligence? For many years people have wondered about it. How do people define it? What affects intelligence more: environment or heredity? How do people measure intelligence? Does intelligence mean success in life? Discuss these questions with your classmates and teacher.

Teachers and psychologists have known for a long time that some people learn some things faster than others. Some people learn certain subjects better than they learn others. One person may be good at math but poor at languages. Another may be good at languages but poor at music. Some people may learn new things fast. Other people may learn them slowly. Questions about learning are part of the study of intelligence. Psychologists have made tests called IQ tests to measure intelligence. They want to explain and define intelligence, to measure it with IQ tests, and to understand the IQ scores.

The definition of intelligence is not universal. Nobody agrees on a definition of intelligence. One definition says intelligence is the ability to deal with new situations. Other definitions include the ability to solve problems. Some say intelligence comes from environment. Environment is the situation people live in. Some definitions say people are born with intelligence. Some say intelligence is a combination of the two: environment and natural ability. People use the words *intelligence* and *intelligent* in many ways. The exact definition is not clear.

Intelligence is difficult to define, but psychologists try to measure it. Information from the IQ test may help some people. Alfred Binet, a Frenchman, began testing intelligence in 1905. Binet and Simon, another psychologist, wanted to find students who would probably succeed and those who would probably not succeed. Their test was revised later by psychologists at Stanford University. The test commonly used today is the Stanford-Binet test. This test is one of the most famous tests of a person's intelligence quotient (IQ). Another popular test today is the Wechsler Intelligence Scale for Children (WISC), and the Wechsler Adult Intelligence Scale (WAIS). There are other intelligence tests. Most of these tests measure memory, definitions, reasoning, drawing analogies, calculation, classification, and several other areas. The scores are calculated in several ways. On the major tests, the average score is 100. If a person scores between 90 and 110, this is usually considered average. Above 130 is usually called gifted. Below 85 usually indicates some learning disability.

What do the scores actually mean? This question is very difficult to answer. Many times the tests show learning problems. Then the students can get help. However, there are several problems with understanding and using the test scores.

First, intelligence changes. A child of five may have a different score than at age 10.

Another problem with the test is the language of the test. If the student's native language is not the same language as the test, the student's score may be low.

An additional problem is culture. American tests are best for middle- and upper-class people. Therefore, other people may have lower scores.

Another problem is "labeling." If a child scores high, people believe that the child will do well in school. If the child does not do well, some people may wrongly believe that the child is lazy or bored. There may be other reasons why the child is not doing well. The opposite problem is also true. Sometimes a child scores low. From that time, some people may expect the child not to do well. Therefore, the child begins to believe that he or she will not do well.

In conclusion, it is difficult to define intelligence, but psychologists try to measure it with IQ tests. These tests are often very helpful because they identify students who may have problems or who may be very intelligent. However, the scores may not be easy to understand. People must be very careful in using the scores. Careful use of the scores can provide a lot of information. Misuse of the scores may cause many problems.

616 words ________ time ________ wpm

MAIN IDEA

Choose the main idea of the article.

a. Not everyone agrees on the definition of intelligence.

b. Alfred Binet was one of the first to test intelligence.

c. It is difficult to define and to measure intelligence.

d. Sometimes test scores can be misused.

Circle the problems with using IQ test scores.

Intelligence cannot be defined.

There are many tests.

Intelligence can change with age.

The student's language must be the same as the test.

The test identifies gifted children.

The test is for certain classes.

Children may be labeled.

The test identifies children who need help.

COMPREHENSION QUESTIONS

Write **T** before true statements. Write **F** before false statements.

_____ 1. Environment may influence intelligence tests.

_____ 2. IQ measures many different mental skills.

_____ 3. Alfred Binet's original test is being used today.

_____ 4. *Someone who scores 145 on an IQ test is very much above average.

_____ 5. The native language of the student has no influence on IQ test scores.

_____ 6. *To give an IQ test to students of English as a second language would probably produce meaningful results.

_____ 7. IQ test scores can be used incorrectly, but they also can provide a lot of good information.

_____ 8. There is only one IQ test available.

_____ 9. *People should use IQ test scores very carefully.

_____ 10. Psychologists agree on a definition for intelligence.

_____ number answered correctly

After correcting your answers, go back to the article to find out why they are correct. Try to discover the meaning of the new words in context.

Write the line number of the sentence that states the main idea of this article. _____

Write the line numbers of the sentence or sentences that support your answers to questions 4 _____, 6 _____, and 10 _____.

VOCABULARY IN CONTEXT

Find the words in the article. The line numbers are in parentheses. Match the definition with the word.

_____ 1. universal (10) — a. the situation people live in

_____ 2. environment (13) — b. everyone agrees

_______ 3. revised (22) c. not the same, different

_______ 4. gifted (32) d. look at again, change

_______ 5. opposite (49) e. above average

ROOTS AND AFFIXES

Look at the examples below. Then answer the questions. This exercise is about roots and affixes in this article and others. Try to discover the meaning of the roots and affixes.

1. I did not *recognize* my friend at the costume party. I did not know who she was.
   Cognitive psychology studies knowledge and how people learn.

   "cogn" means _______________.

2. *Television* is something you see at a distance.
   A *revision* is seeing something again to make it better.
   A *vision* is like a dream. It is something that you see.

   "vis" probably means _______________.

3. A *popular* person is one whom people like.
   The *population* is the number of people.
   In an election, the *populace* votes for the leaders.

   "popul" means _______________.

4. I'm sorry. I *misunderstood* your questions. I didn't understand.
   Mary accidentally *misspelled* the teacher's name. The teacher was not happy.
   Many students *mispronounce* English words at first. It takes time to learn the correct pronunciation.

   "mis" means _______________.

Learn these new stems and prefixes.

cogn	know, learn
vis	see
popul	people
mis	error

Review the roots, prefixes, and suffixes you have studied in this chapter. Match the definitions with the root.

______	1.	anti	a. make
______	2.	cogn	b. against
______	3.	fact	c. error
______	4.	il	d. know
___c___	5.	mis	e. people
___e___	6.	popul	f. not
______	7.	port	h. in favor of
______	8.	pro	i. see
______	9.	simil	j. carry
______	10.	sub, sup	k. not
___m___	11.	un	l. the same
___m___	12.	vari	m. different
______	13.	vis	n. under

PRONOUN REFERENCE

Read these sentences. Some pronouns are italicized. Circle the noun that the pronoun replaces.

1. Teachers and psychologists have known for a long time that some people learn some things faster than *others*.
2. Some people may learn new things fast. Other people may learn *them* slowly.
3. Part of intelligence is an ability to learn. Educational psychologists want to define and measure *it*.
4. One definition says intelligence is the ability to deal with new situations. Some psychologists believe *it* is the ability to solve problems. *Some* say it comes from environment. *Some* say it comes from heredity; some say intelligence is a combination of the *two*.
5. Binet and Simon, other psychologists, wanted to find students who would probably succeed and *those* who would probably not succeed. *Their* test was revised later by psychologists at Stanford University.

QUESTIONS FOR DISCUSSION

1. Did you ever try to train an animal to do something? How did you do it?
2. In the educational system of your country, are there tests for intelligence? Are they used or misused? What is your opinion of intelligence tests?
3. Should all children take intelligence tests? Should only certain children take them? If not all children, which children should take them?

chapter

5

Reading Graphs, Tables, and Charts

lesson 26

Sources of Data

preview Read this article to find out how researchers and companies get information. Did you ever wonder how social scientists or advertising executives make their decisions?

Before the advertising account manager can begin to plan an ad, much research must be done. Who will buy this product? Why do customers buy this product? Advertisers need to know how many people of a certain age or sex live in this city. How can advertisers find this information about people? They do research. Social and behavioral scientists do research also. They need to find information about people. There are many sources of data, and there are many ways to collect data.

In this age of computerization, many databases are available. A database is a large amount of information stored in the computer. There are databases that include information about the stock market, business, and many other fields. After the information is collected, it is loaded into computer memory so that researchers can use it.

One large collection of data is the census. Every ten years the population of the United States is counted. At the same time, the government gathers information about the people. This information includes people's living habits, their spending and saving habits, their educational plans and achievements, and other things. This information helps the government to serve the people. This information can also be used by researchers. It is available in many libraries in the United States.

Another source of data for social science is test scores. There are many kinds of tests: intelligence, aptitude, achievement, personality, and interest inventory. Each of these tests measures a different part of human experience. Social science research can use these tests and their results to describe people in general.

The government collects data during the census, but there are other ways to collect the data. One technique is the survey. This technique is very common, and it has many forms. In a survey, the researcher tries to measure the opinions of people on some subject. Survey information can be collected in several ways.

One kind of survey is the interview. The interviewer asks people several questions about their opinions. The advantage of this is that a researcher can get a lot of information. The disadvantage is that a researcher must spend a lot of time in interviews.

Another kind of survey is by mail. People in the United States often receive mail surveys. A mail survey usually includes a few questions. People fill out the form and send it back. The advantage of this is that a researcher can contact many people. The disadvantage is that many people do not respond. In fact, less than 50 percent of the people usually answer the survey. Another disadvantage is that the researcher cannot get as much information from each person as with an interview.

Some researchers do telephone surveys. This form of survey is becoming more and more popular. The advantage of this is that the researcher can get information quickly. More people probably answer a telephone survey than a mail survey. However, a telephone survey can sometimes be expensive.

It is impossible to ask everyone in a country, state, or city about their opinions. Therefore, a researcher must choose a small group of people to survey. This small group must be similar to the entire population. It is a sample of the population. To survey national opinion in the United States, the sample must include a certain percentage of whites, Blacks, Mexican Americans, and other minorities. The sample must also include people with high, middle, and low incomes. In addition, the sample must include people from the city and the country as well as people from all parts of the country. Choosing a good sample is extremely difficult, but it is necessary to have a good sample for correct survey results.

In the United States, data are collected on two different occasions: to predict the result of elections and to measure the popularity of TV shows. For each election, professional researchers try to find out the opinions of the people. They sample the population. Based on a sample of several thousand, they can predict the winner of the election. In recent presidential elections, researchers successfully predicted the winner. Sometimes, however, predictions are not correct. Researchers once predicted that Franklin Delano Roosevelt would lose. Of course, he did not. The researchers used poor sampling methods in that election. Some people oppose the use of samples to predict the result of elections. They say that the prediction may influence or change the election.

Advertisers want to know which TV shows are more popular. They want to know who watches certain TV shows. A company called Nielsen measures the most popular television shows each week. They do this by contacting a sample of families across the United States to find out which shows they are watching. Each week, this company makes a list of the most popular shows. This is very important to the shows and the advertisers because more popular shows can charge more money to advertisers.

In summary, there are many sources of data. These include computerized databases and test results. There are also many ways to collect data. Surveys, including interviews, mail and telephone surveys, are the most common ways to collect data. In a survey the researcher collects data or opinions from a sample population. The data are used in many ways: for scientific studies, to predict election results, and for advertising.

881 words ________ time ________ wpm

MAIN IDEA

Choose the main idea for this article.

a. There are many sources of data and many ways for researchers to collect data.

b. The United States takes a census survey every ten years and accumulates a great deal of data about the people.

c. Only 50 percent of the people usually respond to a mail survey.

d. Some people say that predicting the winners of presidential elections may change the election.

Circle six sources of data

the U.S. census

advertising

tests

interviews

television

mail survey

telephone survey

presidential election

databases

COMPREHENSION QUESTIONS

Write **T** before true statements and **F** before false statements. Do not look at the article.

_____ 1. Social scientists are the only people who need to find information about people.

_____ 2. The U.S. government counts the population and collects data about the people every twenty-five years.

_____ 3. Test scores do not give data about people.

_____ 4. *In an interview, the interviewer talks to each person individually.

_____ 5. *Interviews usually provide more information than mail surveys.

_______ 6. *A researcher can get information more quickly from a telephone survey than from a mail survey.

_______ 7. A sample population is a small group that is similar to the whole population.

_______ 8. It is easy to choose a sample population for a survey.

_______ 9. Surveys can usually predict the results of elections.

_______ 10. *If a TV show is not popular, the advertiser will continue to advertise on that show.

_______ number answered correctly

After correcting your answers, go back to the article and find out why the answers are correct. Try to discover the meanings of new words from the context.

Write the line number of the sentence that states the main idea of this article. _________

Write the line numbers of the sentence or sentences that support your answer to questions 4 _________, 5 _________, 6 _________, and 10 _________.

SUBJECT-VERB IDENTIFICATION

Read these sentences from the article. Identify the main subject and the main verb. Underline the subject one time; underline the verb twice. Some of the sentences are passive. Underline the complete verb and identify the doer of the action.

1. Before the advertising account manager can begin to plan an ad, much research must be done.
2. After the information is collected, it is loaded into computer memory for researchers to use.
3. This information can also be used by researchers.
4. Each of these tests measures a different part of human experience.
5. This technique is very common, and it has many forms.
6. The disadvantage is that a researcher must spend a lot of time in interviews.

7. To survey national opinion in the United States, the sample must include a certain percentage of whites, Blacks, Mexican Americans, and other minorities.
8. In addition, the sample must include people from the city and the country as well as people from all parts of the country.
9. Choosing a good sample is extremely difficult.
10. It is necessary to have a good sample for correct survey results.

CLOZE

Fill in the spaces with any word that completes the meaning. Use grammar and vocabulary clues to help you. Do not go back to the article.

One kind of survey is the interview. The interviewer ____________ people several questions about ____________ opinions. The advantage of ____________ is that a researcher ____________ get a lot of information. ____________ disadvantage is ____________ a researcher must spend ____________ lot of time in ____________.

Another kind of survey ____________ by mail. People in ____________ United States often receive ____________ surveys. A mail survey usually ____________ a few questions. People ____________ out the form and ____________ it back. The advantage ____________ this is that a ____________ can contact many people. ____________ disadvantage is that many ____________ do not respond. In ____________, less than 50 percent of the people usually answer ____________ survey. Another disadvantage is that the researcher cannot get as much information from each person as with an interview.

DISCUSSION QUESTIONS

1. How could predictions influence or change an important election?
2. Have you ever collected data for a research project? Tell the class about your experience.
3. Think of some information you would like to know about Americans. Prepare a few short questions. Ask a number of Americans. What can you say about your results?

lesson 27

Statistics–Measures of Central Tendency

preview Read this article to learn about three useful statistics used by researchers.

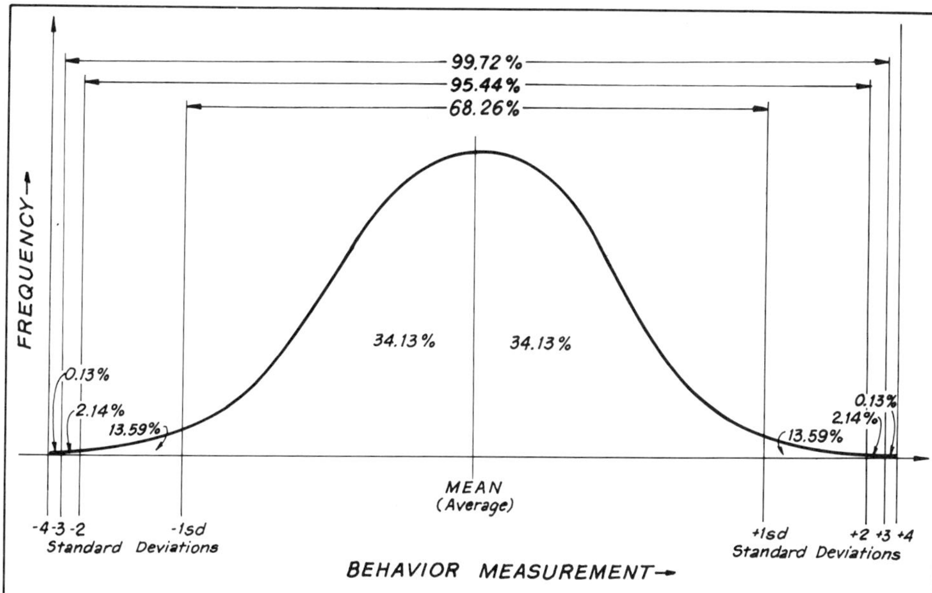

NORMAL DISTRIBUTION CURVE WITH STANDARD DEVIATIONS AND PERCENTAGES

A teacher often asks "How did the class do on the test?" When a teacher asks this question, he or she wants information about the entire class. There are three *statistics* which answer this question. These statistics are the measures of central tendency. Their purpose is to describe group performance with one number. Measures of central tendency are used for research, education and business. The three measures of central tendency are the mean, the median, and the mode.

The *mean* is a very common and very useful statistic. It is the arithmetic average. The mean is a number that describes a group, or sample. It is easy to compute the mean. First, add all the data in the sample, then divide by the number of subjects. For example, ten students take a test, and they earn these scores: 100, 98, 96, 95, 89, 83, 82, 74, 70, and 65. First, add the scores. The total of the ten scores is 852. Second, divide by the sample size, which is 10 in this example. The mean for this sample is $852 \div 10 = 85.2$. If a teacher wants one number to represent, or describe, the entire class of ten students, the number is 85.2. The symbol for the mean is $\overline{x}$. For this example, a statistician writes $\overline{x} = 85.2$.

Although the mean is a useful statistic, the *median* is another useful measure of central tendency. The median, which is abbreviated *Mdn*, divides the data into two equal halves, 50 percent above the median and 50 percent below. To find the median, first it is necessary to arrange the scores from highest to lowest. As an example, consider these test scores:

Student	*Score*
1	99
2	95
3	74
4	73
5	71

The median for these scores is 74. Exactly half of the scores are above and half below, except for the one score which falls on the median. However, the mean ($\overline{x}$) for these scores is $(99 + 95 + 74 + 73 + 71)/5 = 82.4$. The two high scores, 99 and 95 influence the mean but not the median. As a result, people sometimes use the median if there are very high or low scores in a group of scores. This is an important advantage of the median.

A third descriptive statistic is the *mode*. The mode is the score that happens most often. Look at the scores below:

Subject	*Score*
1	99
2	98
3	85
4	83
5	83
6	83
7	81
8	70
9	63
10	59

Three students have a score of 83. This score is the most frequent score. Therefore, the mode is 83. The mode is easy to identify, but statisticians do not often use the mode. Compared to the mean and the median, the mode is clearly less useful.

In summary, there are three measures of central tendency: the mean, median, and mode. The calculations for each one are different, and each one has slightly different uses.

501 words ________ time ________ wpm

MAIN IDEA

Choose the main idea for this article.

a. The mean is the arithmetic average.

b. The median is the midpoint.

c. The mode is the score that occurs most often.

d. The mean, median, and mode are three measures of central tendency.

COMPREHENSION QUESTIONS

Write **T** before true statements and **F** before false statements. *Do not* look back at the reading.

______ 1. The mean, median, and mode are not useful.

______ 2. The arithmetic average is the same as the median.

______ 3. The median is more useful if there are extremely low scores in a group of scores.

______ 4. *If a teacher tells a class the mean score of a test, it helps each student to understand his or her score better.

______ 5. *The mean and median are never the same numbers.

______ 6. *The mean and the mode are the same.

______ 7. The mode is the most common measure of central tendency.

______ 8. The median is the middle score.

______ 9. $\bar{x}$ is the mode.

______ 10. 10, 9, 9, 9, 8, 8, 6, 5, 4
The mode for these scores is 8.

______ number answered correctly

After correcting your answers, go back to the text to see why they are correct. Use the context to understand the meaning of new words.

Write the line number of the sentence that states the main idea of this article. ________

Write the line numbers of the sentence or sentences that support your answer to questions 4 ________, 5 ________, and 6 ________.

PROBLEMS TO SOLVE

1. Look at the following test scores and answer the questions that follow.

Subject	*Score*
1	10
2	9
3	7
4	5
5	4
6	4
7	3

   a. what is the mean?
   b. What is the median?
   c. What is the mode?

2. The mean of a student's three test scores is 75. The score on the first test is 70. The score on the second test is 75. What is the score on the third test?
3. The median of a group of 50 scores is 70. How many people earned a score above 70?
4. The average daily high temperature for the month of August in Tucson is 95°F. How is this average calculated?

QUESTIONS FOR DISCUSSION

1. Which statistic is better to use for reporting salary, or income, of a group of people? Remember that some people earn extremely high salaries.
2. The mean of a group of test scores is 85. The median for the same group of scores is 70. Why is the mean higher?

READING CHARTS

To analyze your own progress and improvement in reading, look at chapter 5, lesson 35 on page 218. Analyze your own Personal Progress Charts.

lesson 28

Bar Graphs

preview Very often scientists and business people need to present a lot of information. Sometimes the information is easier to read and understand in a graph, chart, or table. There are different kinds of graphs: bar graph, line graph, and pie graph (circle chart). In the next few lessons you will learn how to read graphs, charts, and tables.

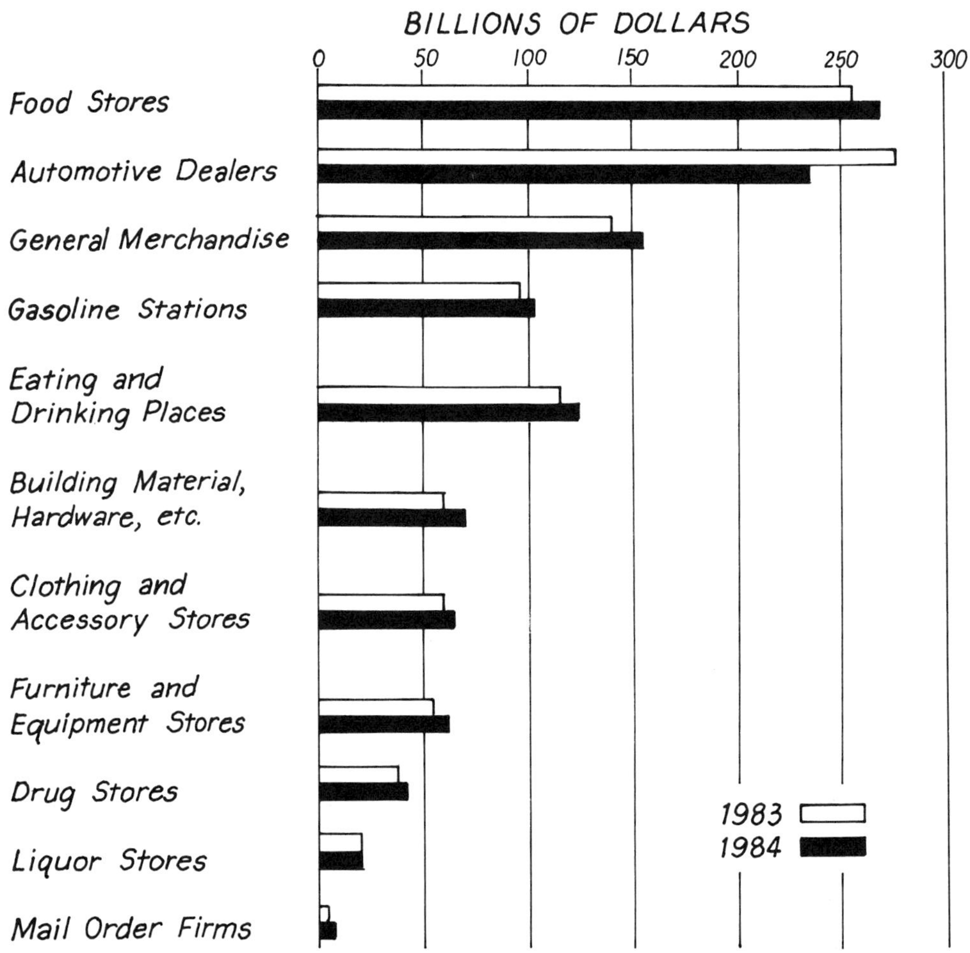

SOURCE: U.S. Bureau of the Census, Statistical Abstract of the United States: 1986 (106th Edition) Washington, D.C., 1985

FIGURE 1 RETAIL STORE SALES

When reading a bar graph, you must understand several things. First look at the title. This tells you the subject of the graph. Second, look at the horizontal and the vertical axes (singular axis). The horizontal axis goes across the page, and the vertical axis goes up and down. These are also called the abscissa and the ordinate. Look carefully to see which data are on each axis. One variable is on each axis. Third look at the scale on each axis. What does each division on the axis represent? It is important to notice this. Finally, look at the source. This tells you where the data came from. The source is often at the bottom of the graph.

Look at Figure 1. Look at the title. This graph tells the dollar amount of sales for different kinds of retail stores for two years: 1983 and 1984. Notice that the vertical axis (up and down) represents each kind of retail store, and that each kind of store has two bars. The white bar represents 1983 and the black bar represents 1984. See the key in the bottom right-hand corner. The horizontal axis (across the page) represents retail sales in billions of dollars. Therefore, when the graph says 50 on the horizontal axis, it means 50 billion (50,000,000,000). This kind of abbreviation is often used for large numbers. Finally, look at the source of the data. This graph was prepared by the U.S. Bureau of the Census.

It is possible to make comparisons by using this graph. The same kind of retail store can be compared for the two years. Different kinds of retail stores can be compared. For example, sales of automotive dealers descreased from 1983 to 1984, from 280 billion to 230 billion. This was the only kind of store in which sales decreased. Also, furniture stores sold more than drug stores in both years. Mail-order houses sold less than all others in both years.

It is often necessary to make generalizations and inferences from graphs. These are some of the generalizations you can make from this graph. From 1983 to 1984, all sales increased except automotive dealer sales. It is possible that 1983 was a good year, or 1984 was an "off" year for auto dealers. Gasoline service stations sales increased very little. Researchers may use these data to make inferences about the economy. More money was spent on food and autos than on all other goods. This might show something about how people spend their money. Most sales increased at about the same rate. This might indicate something about economic growth.

PRACTICE WITH BAR GRAPHS

Look at Figure 2 and answer these questions.

1. For each graph, what information is on the horizontal axis?
2. For each graph, what information is on the vertical axis?
3. Which ten years had the least immigration, according to the graph? Which graph answers this question?
4. What ten-year period had the most immigration?
5. How many immigrants for each 1,000 Americans were there between 1920 and 1930?
6. Are these two graphs different or the same?
7. From 1880 to 1890, how many people immigrated to the United States?
8. From 1970 to 1980, how many people immigrated to the United States?
9. From these graphs, can you tell from which countries immigrants came?
10. Approximately how many immigrants were there from 1900 to 1930?

List as many generalizations from this data as you can.

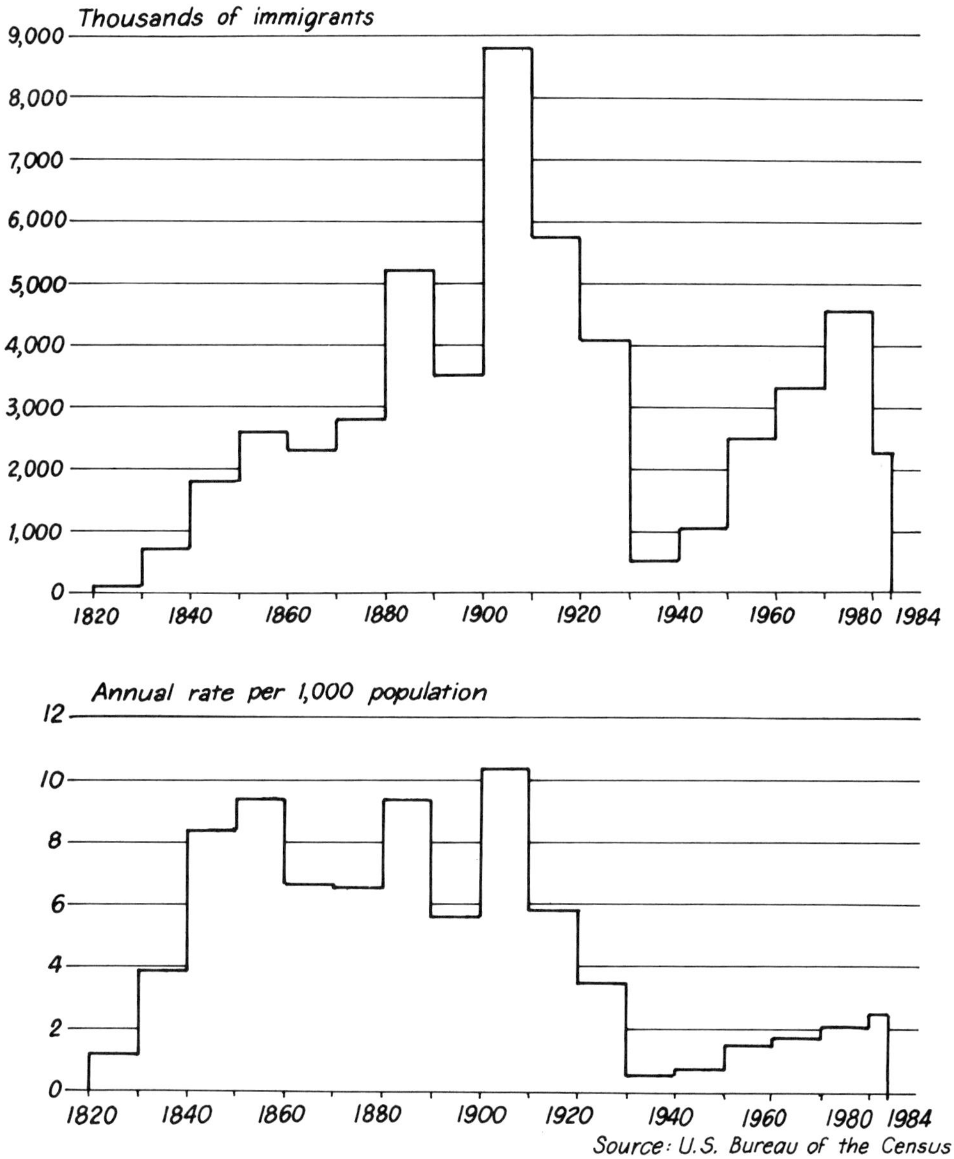

FIGURE 2 IMMIGRATION 1820 TO 1984

Source: U.S. Bureau of the Census, Statistical Abstract of the United States: 1986 (106th ed.), Washington, D.C., 1985, p. 82.

CONSTRUCT YOUR OWN GRAPH

Draw a bar graph. Show the number of students in your class or school from each country. If there are many countries represented, divide the world into geographic areas: North America, South America, Europe, Africa, and Asia. If all the students are from one country, then divide the country into cities, states, or provinces.

List as many generalizations from this data as you can.

lesson 29

Circle Graphs

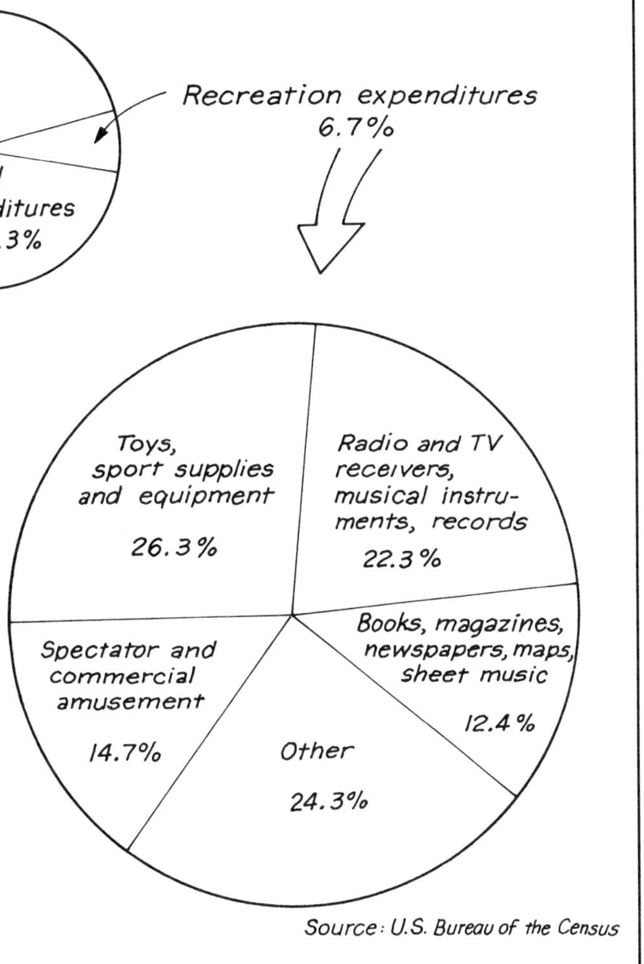

FIGURE 3 PERSONAL EXPENDITURES FOR RECREATION, 1984

Source: U.S Bureau of the Census, Statistical Abstract of the United States: 1986 (106th ed.), Washington, D.C., 1985, p. 222.

Circle graphs show percentages or proportions of a whole. They show exactly what percentage each item takes of 100 percent. Another name for a circle graph is "pie graph" because the graph looks like a pie, something that you eat for dessert, cut into pieces.

To read a pie graph, look at the title first. It tells the subject of the graph or what is represented by the 100 percent. Second, look at the parts, or slices, of the pie. Each triangular shape represents a percentage of the whole. The percentage is represented by the size of the piece.

PRACTICE WITH CIRCLE GRAPHS

Look at Figure 3 on page 199 and answer the questions.

1. Restate the title in a complete sentence that shows its meaning.
2. What is the source of these data?
3. In the smaller pie, what does the number 6.7 percent represent?
4. How does this 6.7 percent relate to the larger pie?
5. What percentage of recreational expenditures is made on toys?
6. What percentage of recreational expenditure is made on books, magazines, newspapers, spectator, and commercial amusement?
7. In the pie that shows recreational expenditures, what do you think the category "other" includes? (24.3%)
8. In the small pie, what do you think "other" means?

List as many generalizations as you can make from this graph.

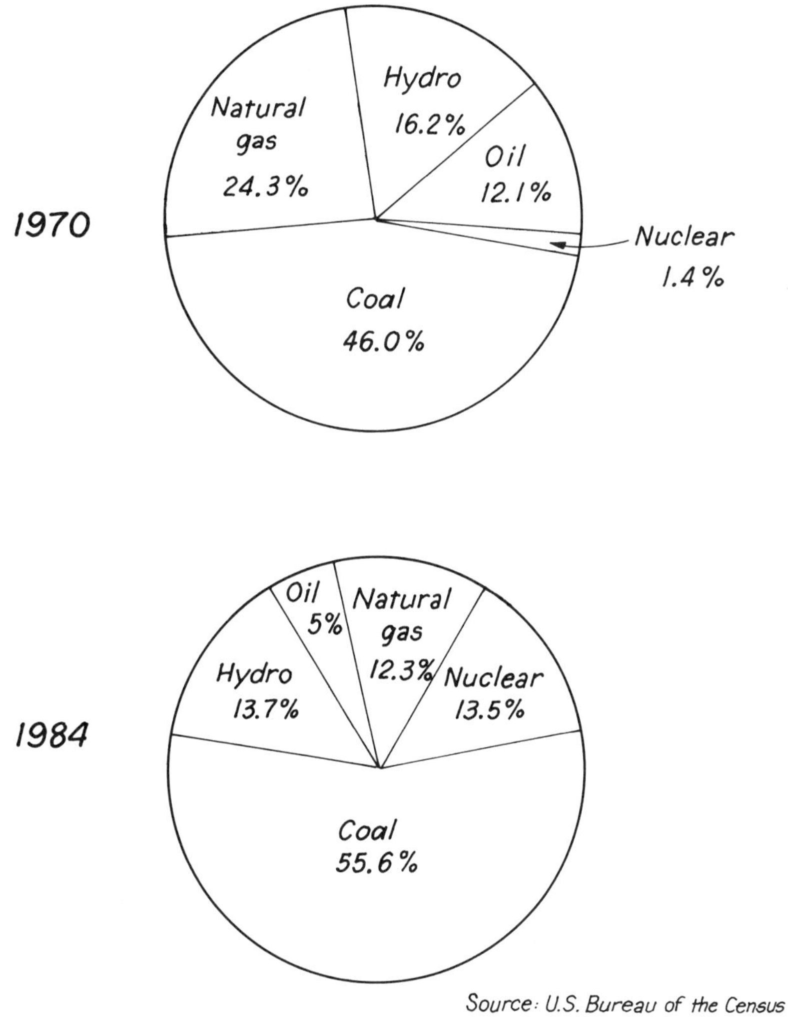

FIGURE 4 ELECTRIC ENERGY PRODUCTION BY SOURCE OF ENERGY

Source: U.S Bureau of the Census, Statistical Abstract of the United States: 1986 (106th ed.), Washington, D.C., 1985, p. xxviii.

Look at Figure 4 on page 201 and answer the questions.

1. Look at the title. What does this graph show?
2. Restate the title in a complete sentence.
3. What do the two pies represent? How are they different?
4. How many times did the use of nuclear energy increase between 1970 and 1984?
5. Did the use of coal for electricity increase or decrease between 1970 and 1984?
6. Which sources of electricity were used less in 1984 than in 1970?
7. What was the most important source of energy in 1970? in 1984?
8. What happened to the use of gas and oil?

List as many generalizations as you can make from this graph.

CONSTRUCT YOUR OWN GRAPH

Draw a circle graph of your monthly personal expenditures. The circle will represent your total monthly income. You may divide the circle into the following: rent, utilities (including gas, electric, water, garbage, and telephone), food, clothes, school expenses (including tuition or books), and entertainment. You may use amounts of money or percentage of money in your circle.

lesson
30

Line Graphs

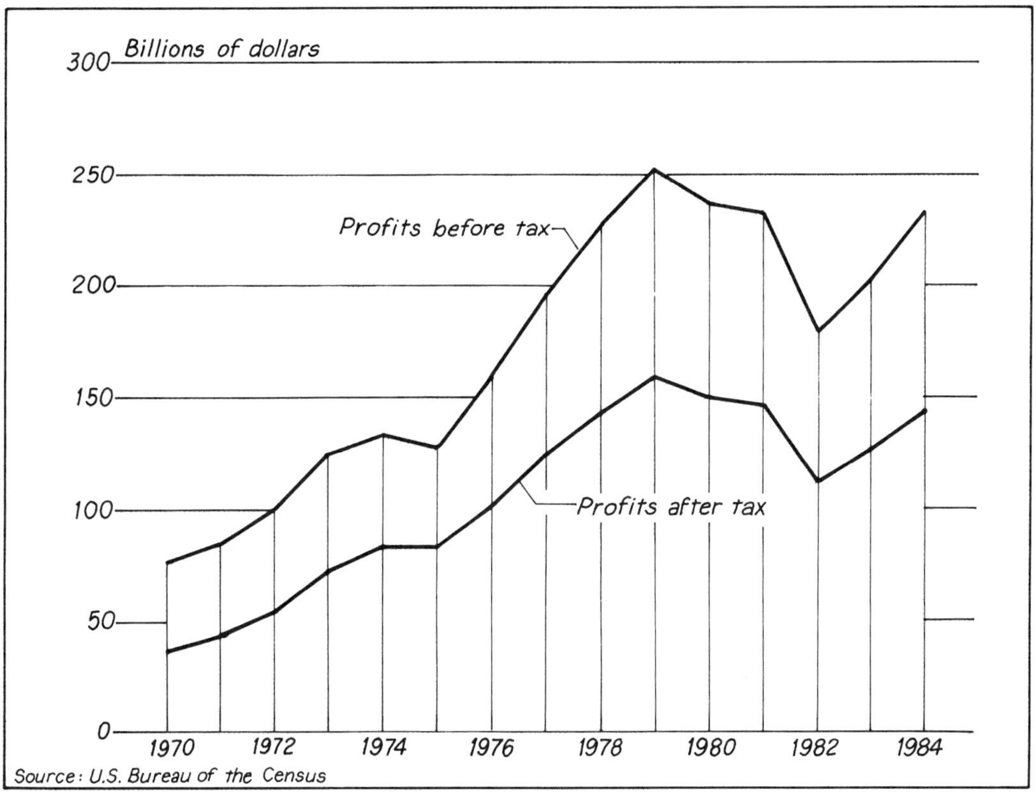

FIGURE 5 CORPORATE PROFITS: 1970 TO 1984

Source: U.S. Bureau of the Census, Statistical Abstract of the United States: 1986 (106th ed.), Washington, D.C., 1985, p. 514

Line graphs are similar to bar graphs, but they use a line to connect the points on the graph. Like bar graphs, they have a title, horizontal and vertical axes, and a source. Each axis has a scale. It is necessary to note what each division on the scale represents. A line graph is very good for showing things that happen over a period of time. For example, Figure 2, the bar graph about immigration from 1820 through 1984, can also be drawn as a line graph.

PRACTICE WITH LINE GRAPHS

Look at Figure 5 on page 203 and answer the following questions.

1. Look at the title and restate it in a complete sentence.
2. What does each division on the vertical axis represent?
3. What does each division on the horizontal axis represent?
4. Look at the two horizontal lines on the graph. The bottom line is tax liability. This is the money the corporation has to pay the government in taxes. What does the other line represent?
5. How much profit did the corporations earn in 1980 before taxes?
6. What was the dollar amount of their actual profit (after tax) in 1980?
7. Is it possible to compare profits from 1984 with those of 1970? How do they compare?
8. What happened to profits in 1982?
9. Have profits been increasing or decreasing since 1970?

List as many generalizations about this graph as you can.

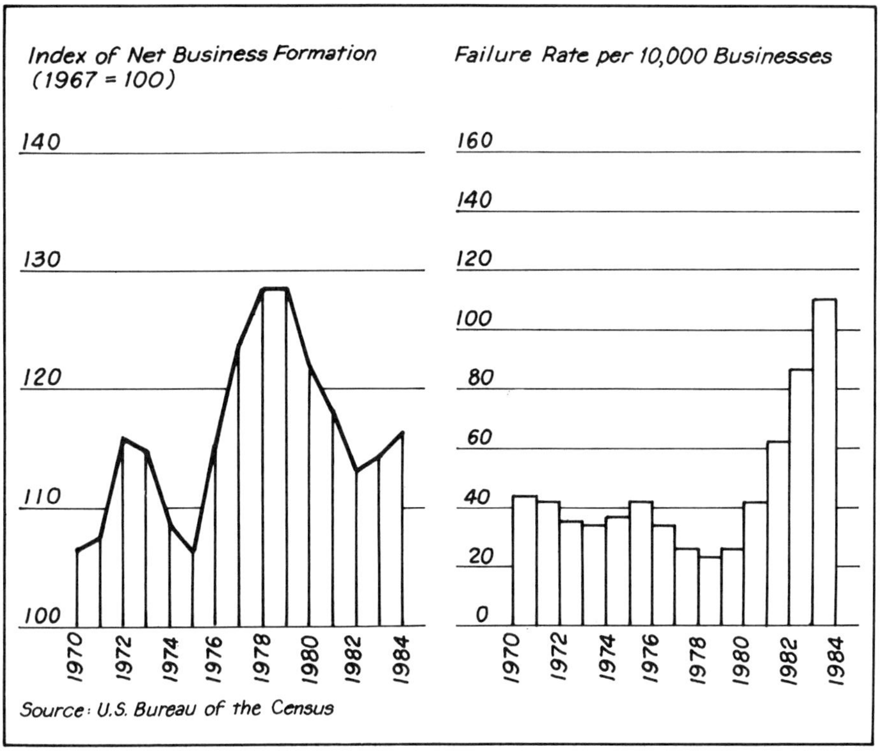

FIGURE 6 INDEX OF NET BUSINESS FORMATION AND BUSINESS FAILURE RATE: 1970 TO 1984

Source: U.S. Bureau of the Census, Statistical Abstract of the United States: 1986 (106th ed.), Washington, D.C., 1985, p. 514

Look at Figure 6 and answer the following questions.

1. Restate the title in a complete sentence.
2. What years are covered on the graph?
3. What does the line graph show?
4. What do the units on the vertical axis represent? What does "index (1967 = 100)" mean?
5. In which years were the most businesses started up?
6. What does the bar graph show?

7. What do the units on the vertical axis represent? What does "rate per 10,000 businesses" mean?
8. Which three years combined had the most failures?
9. Which three years has the least failures?
10. What is the relationship between the two graphs?

List as many generalizations as you can about this graph.

CONSTRUCT YOUR OWN GRAPH

Listen to the TV weather reports for five days or more, or read the weather section of the newspaper for five days. Then draw a line graph showing the high temperatures for each day. Next, do the same thing for the low temperatures on the same graph.

Combination Graphs

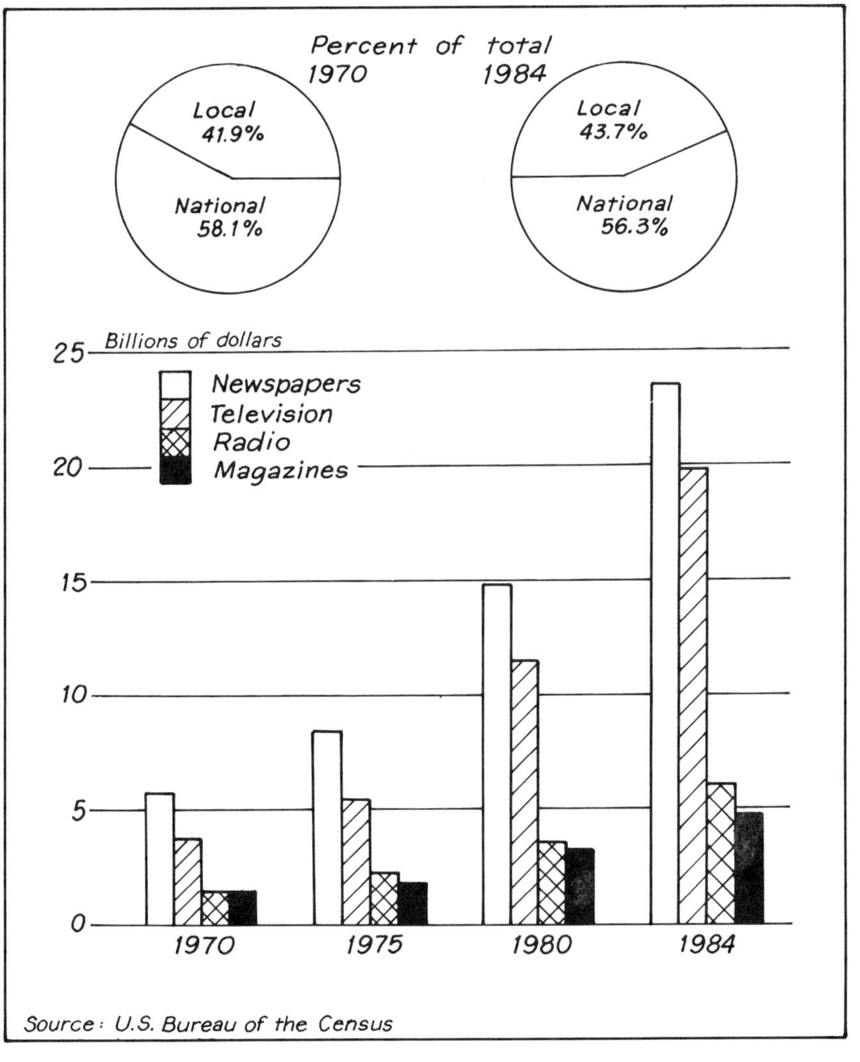

FIGURE 7 ADVERTISING EXPENDITURES BY SELECTED MEDIA: 1970 TO 1984

It is sometimes necessary to use a combination of bar, line, or circle graphs to show related information. The process for understanding these graphs is basically the same. It is necessary to understand the title and the scales on the abscissa and ordinate axes. Finally, check the source of the data.

PRACTICE WITH COMBINATION GRAPHS

Look at Figure 7. It is a combination graph. You can see that it includes a bar graph and a circle graph. Look at the title, the key in the upper left-hand corner, the absscissa, the ordinate, and the source. Then answer the questions.

1. Restate the title in a complete sentence.
2. What does the bar graph show?
3. What does the pie graph show?
4. What information is on the horizontal axis? the vertical axis?
5. What does the number 25 represent at the top of the ordinate?
6. Which medium spent the most money for advertising in 1975?
7. In which year did the radio and magazines spend about the same amount?
8. What conclusions or generalizations can you make about the bar graph?

CONSTRUCT YOUR OWN GRAPH

Make a line graph that shows the growth of human population. Use the data below.

Year	*Population Estimate*	*Year*	*Population Estimate*
1000	340,000,000	1950	2,509,000,000
1650	545,000,000	1970	3,650,000,000
1800	907,000,000	1982	4,600,000,000
1900	1,610,000,000		

lesson 32

Organizational Charts

An organizational chart shows levels of an organization. The top of the chart shows the leadership (the president, director, and so on). The organizational chart of a company might look like this.

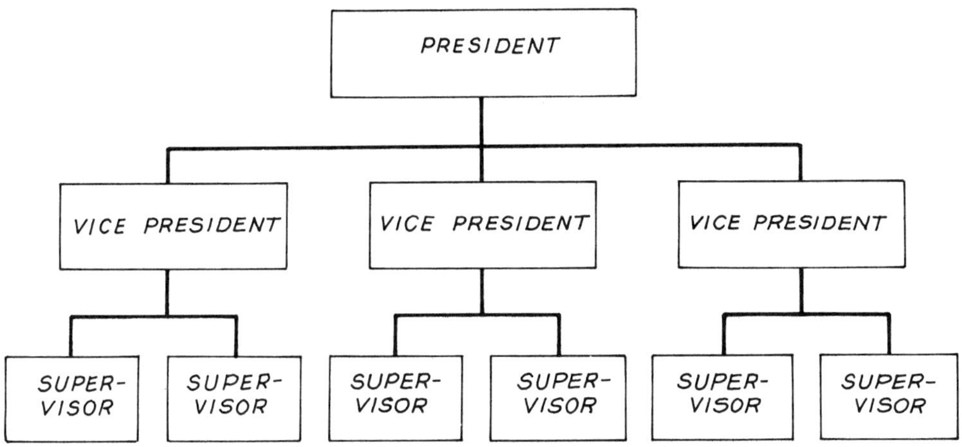

FIGURE 8 LEVELS OF MANAGEMENT

Blocks on the same level are generally equal. In other words, the three vice presidents are equal to each other, and the supervisors are equal to other supervisors. The bottom of the chart shows the lowest levels of the organization.

PRACTICE WITH ORGANIZATIONAL CHARTS

Figure 9 shows the structure or organization of the United States government. Look at a chart carefully and answer the questions.

1. The government of the United States has three branches. What governs, or controls, all three branches?
2. According to the chart, are the three branches (legislative, executive, and judicial) equal in power?
3. Which branch of government is the Department of Agriculture part of?
4. Which branch of government is the Library of Congress part of?
5. Does the United States Supreme Court report directly to the President? How do you know?
6. The Department of State has a leader called the Secretary of State. To whom does the Secretary of State report?

Make as many generalizations about this data as you can.

CONSTRUCT YOUR OWN GRAPH

Draw a chart that shows the organization of your school, institute, company or business.

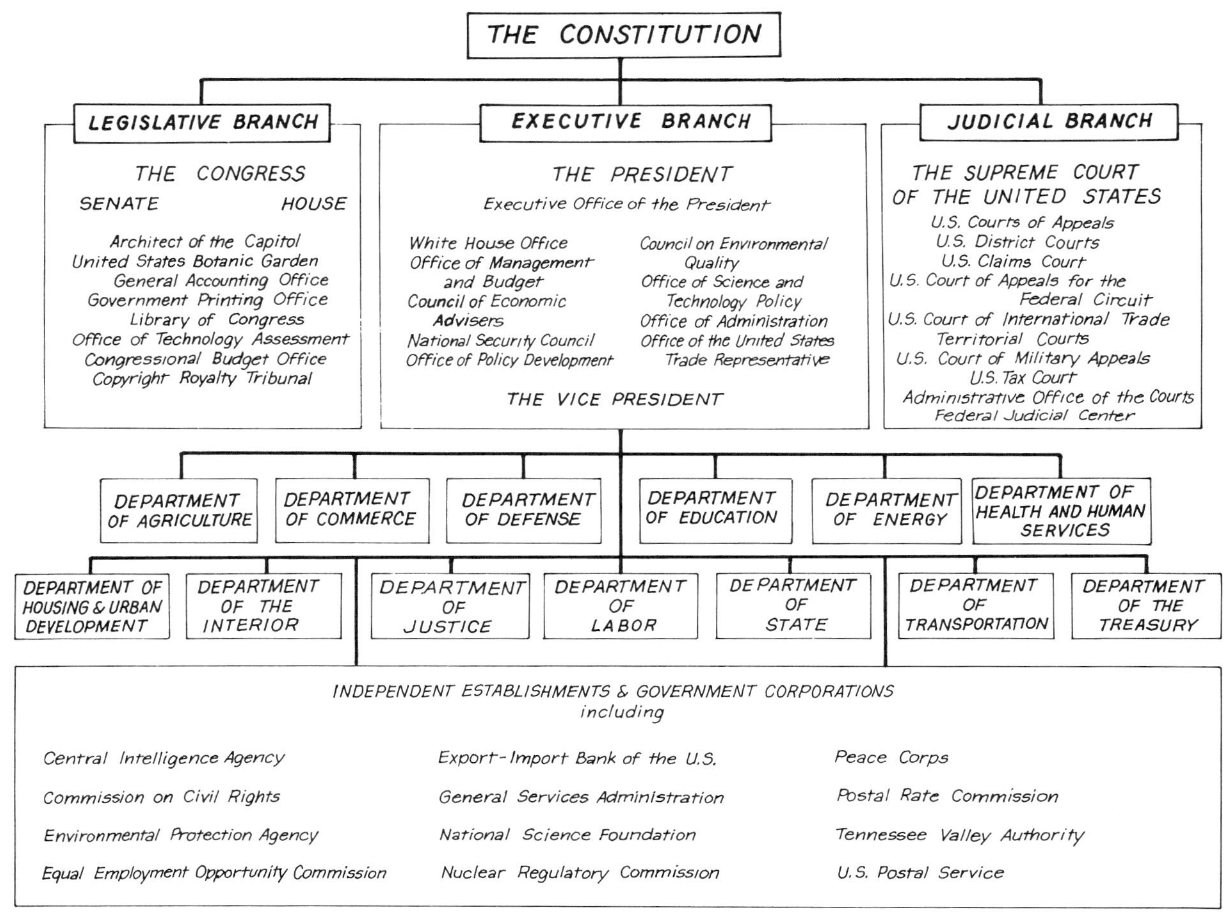

FIGURE 9 THE GOVERNMENT OF THE UNITED STATES

Source: U.S. Bureau of the Census, Statistical Abstract of the United States: 1986 (106th ed.), Washington, D.C., 1985, p. 303.

lesson 33

Reading Maps

Some maps combine geography with other data. These maps are another kind of graph or chart. They show some information that cannot be shown by charts or graphs. Figure 10 is a good example of how maps can be used to show the geographic distribution of data.

PRACTICE WITH MAPS

Look at Figure 10 and answer the following questions.

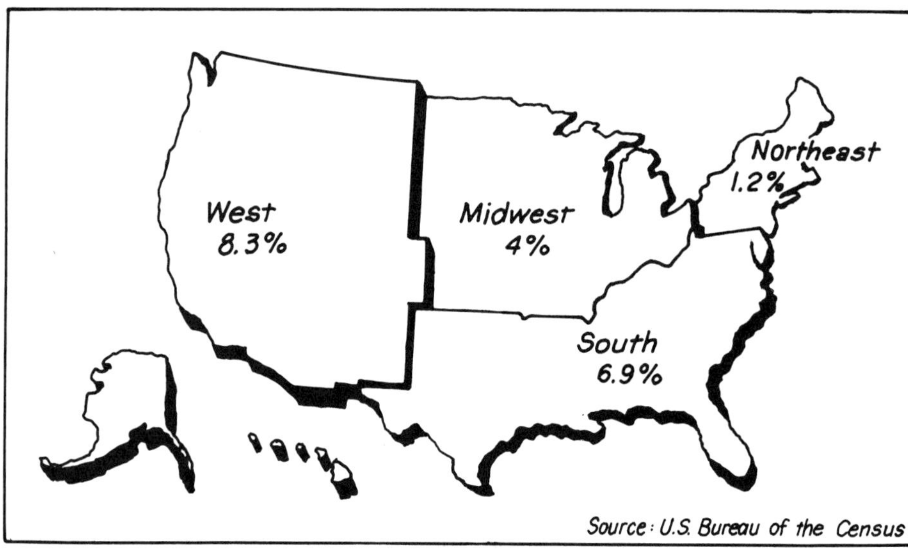

FIGURE 10 RESIDENT POPULATION PERCENT CHANGE 1980 TO 1984

Source: U.S. Bureau of the Census, Statistical Abstract of the United States: 1986 (106th ed.), Washington, D.C., 1985, p. xvii.

1. What is the title of this map?
2. What years are covered in these statistics?
3. What does this map show?

4. Which part of the country grew the fastest during these years?
5. Which part of the country grew the slowest during these years?
6. From this map, can we tell which area has the most people?

Make as many generalizations about this map as you can.

Look at Figure 11 on page 214 and answer these questions.

1. What is the title of this map? Restate the title in a complete sentence.
2. How many original states were there?
3. Where are the original states located?
4. The small dates with the name of the state tell when each state became a state. What were the last two states to become states? When?
5. Are American Samoa, Guam, Puerto Rico, and the Virgin Islands states?
6. What does this map tell you about the direction of U.S. growth?
7. What is the largest amount of land to come into the United States? When did this occur?
8. There is a difference between these words. If you don't know their meaning, look them up in the dictionary.

   original

   acquire

   cede

   annex

   purchase

9. What was the last territory acquired by the United States in any manner? How was it acquired?

Make as many generalizations about this map as you can.

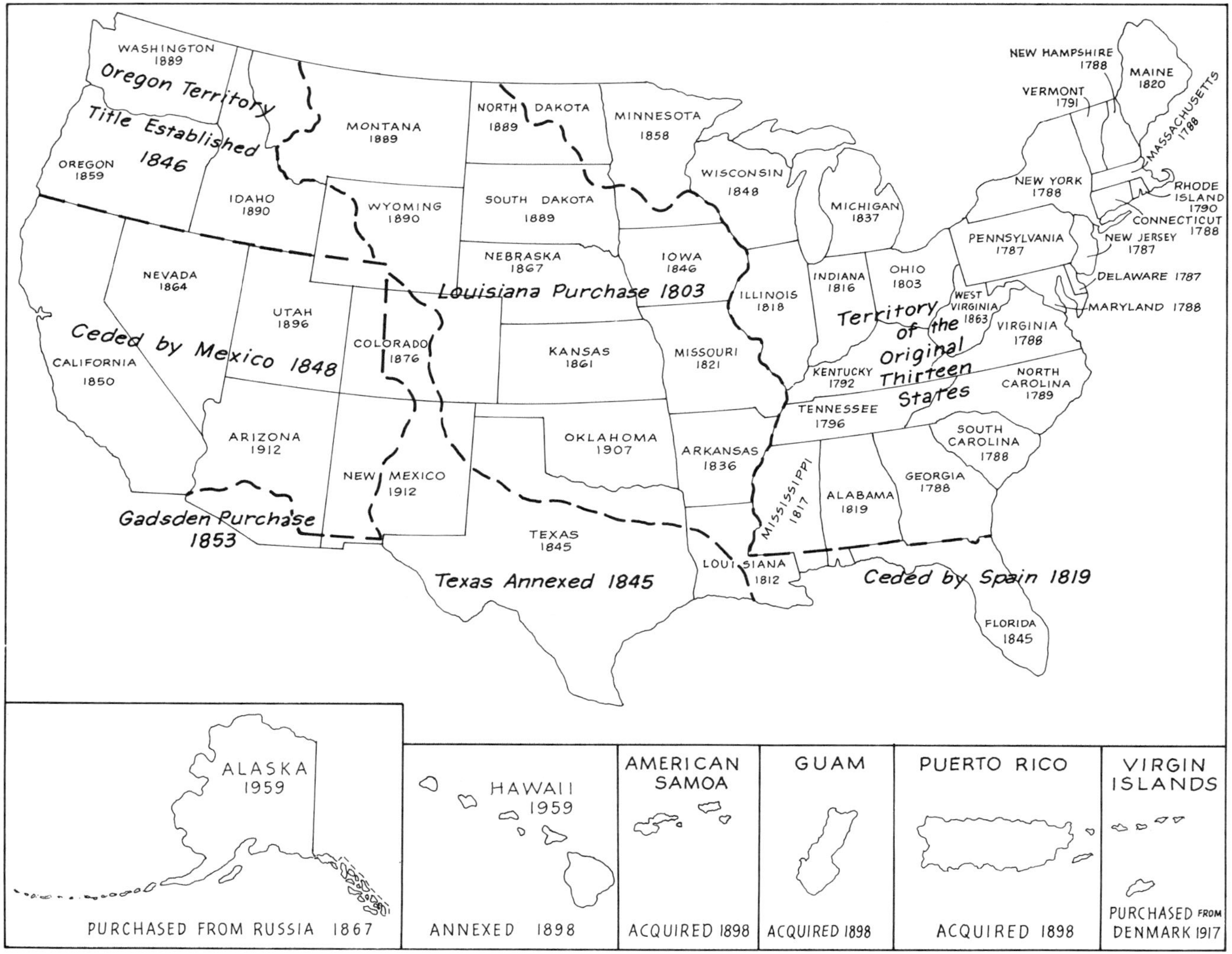

FIGURE 11 TERRITORIAL EXPANSION OF THE UNITED STATES

Source: U.S. Bureau of the Census, Statistical Abstract of the United States: 1986 (106th ed.), Washington, D.C., 1985, p. 193.

CONSTRUCT YOUR OWN GRAPH

Read about your country in an encyclopedia such as the *World Book* or *Book of Knowledge*. Draw a map and combination graph showing important facts about your country. You might include some of the following facts.

population distribution

agricultural production

important resource deposits and mines

lesson 34

Reading Tables

Tables allow researchers and writers to show a lot of information in an easy-to-read format. To explain or tell all of these ideas would take many paragraphs. Reading tables is a little different from reading graphs. Like bar and line graphs, tables have vertical and horizontal directions, but they are not called axes. The horizontal parts of a table are *rows*; the vertical parts of tables are *columns*. The rows and columns have titles that are called headings. At the bottom of the columns, important totals are often given. Like other graphs, tables also have titles and sources and often use abbreviations. Many tables contain footnotes at the bottom. Footnotes give more information about parts of the table. There is a small number in the table that is repeated at the bottom of the table. The explanation is with the small number at the bottom of the table.

FIGURE 12 U.S. SCHOOL ENROLLMENT, 1955 TO 1982, WITH PROJECTIONS TO 1992, AND NUMBER OF SCHOOLS, 1955 TO 1978

(In thousands)

ITEM AND YEAR	TOTAL		ELEMENTARY[1]		SECONDARY		COLLEGE		INDEPENDENT NURSERY AND KINDERGARTEN	
	Public	Private	Public	Private	Public	Private	Public	Private	Public	Private
Enrollment:[2]										
1955	32,164	5,777	22,159	3,800	8,521	800	1,484	1,177	NA	NA
1961	39,793	7,532	24,603	4,900	12,861	1,100	2,329	1,532	NA	NA
1965	46,144	8,251	26,670	4,900	15,504	1,400	3,970	1,951	305	799
1970	52,337	7,516	27,501	4,052	18,408	1,311	6,428	2,153	421	1,106
1975	53,626	7,350	25,640	3,700	19,151	1,300	8,835	2,350	480	1,357
1980	50,444	7,602	24,156	3,623	16,831	1,339	9,457	2,640	632	1,434
1981	49,746	7,824	23,819	3,700	16,280	1,400	9,647	2,724	NA	NA
1982	49,339	7,830	23,865	3,700	15,778	1,400	9,696	2,730	NA	NA
1985, proj	48,568	7,656	23,581	3,600	15,396	1,400	9,591	2,656	NA	NA
1990, proj	49,367	7,795	25,907	4,000	13,962	1,200	9,498	2,595	NA	NA
1992, proj	50,362	7,826	26,785	4,100	14,293	1,200	9,284	2,526	NA	NA
Schools:										
1955	x	x	104.4	12.4	26.0	3.9	0.7	1.2	NA	NA
1961	x	x	81.9	14.8	25.4	4.1	0.7	1.3	NA	NA
1965	x	x	73.2	15.3	26.6	4.6	0.8	1.4	NA	NA
1970	x	x	65.8	14.4	25.4	3.8	1.1	1.5	NA	NA
1978	x	x	62.0	16.1	24.5	5.8	1.5	1.7	NA	NA

NA Not available
X Not applicable
[1] Enrollment includes kindergarten
[2] For regular schools

Source: U.S. Bureau of the Census, Statistical Abstract of the United States: 1986 (106th ed.), Washington, D.C., 1985, p. 126.

PRACTICE WITH TABLES

Look at Figure 12. Read the table. First, look at the title, then look at the headings for the rows and columns. Only after you do these two things will the numbers begin to mean something to you. Answer these questions about Figure 12.

1. What is the title of this table? Restate the title in a complete sentence,
2. This table shows two separate things. What are they?
3. Enrollment is the number of students in a school. The first entry in the table is 32,164. Does it represent 32,164 students, 32,164,000 students, or 32,164,000,000 students?
4. In the headings for the rows, what do you think "proj" means?
5. Public schools are government schools, and students who attend them do not pay tuition. In private schools, students must pay tuition. After looking at this table, what can you say about the number of students in public schools compared with the number of students in private schools? What kind of school has more students?
6. Look at the footnotes at the bottom of the table. What do the abbreviations "NA" and "X" mean?
7. Do elementary schools include kindergarten?
8. Has the number of public elementary schools increased or decreased since 1955?
9. Have private elementary schools increased or decreased since 1955? Explain how you found the answers to these questions.
10. To whom is this table important?

Make as many generalizations about this table as you can.

lesson 35

Analyzing Your Own Charts

After you have completed chapter 5 and several of the other units, answer these questions about your Personal Progress Charts (Figures 13 and 14).

1. Look at your reading speed (wpm). Did you improve?
2. Look at your comprehension score. Was your comprehension score above the satisfactory level in most readings? Did you improve? Improvement can take many forms. If your comprehension score remained above 70 percent and your speed increased, this is improvement. If your comprehension score started low but ended high, this is also improvement, even if speed remained constant. If both speed and comprehension increased, this is a great improvement! If you read the more difficult readings at the same speed and comprehension as the easier readings, this is improvement.
3. What was your average speed on the first three lessons?
4. What was your average speed on the last three lessons?
5. In what chapters did you do the best?
6. In what chapters did you do the worst? Try to figure out why these units caused you problems. How will you deal with these problems in the future? Discuss this question with your teacher.
7. What is your strong point in reading? main idea, inference, vocabulary?
8. What is your weak point in reading? Discuss with your teacher how you can improve in this area.
9. One of the purposes of this text is to help improve your vocabulary. Discuss other ways of doing this with your teacher.

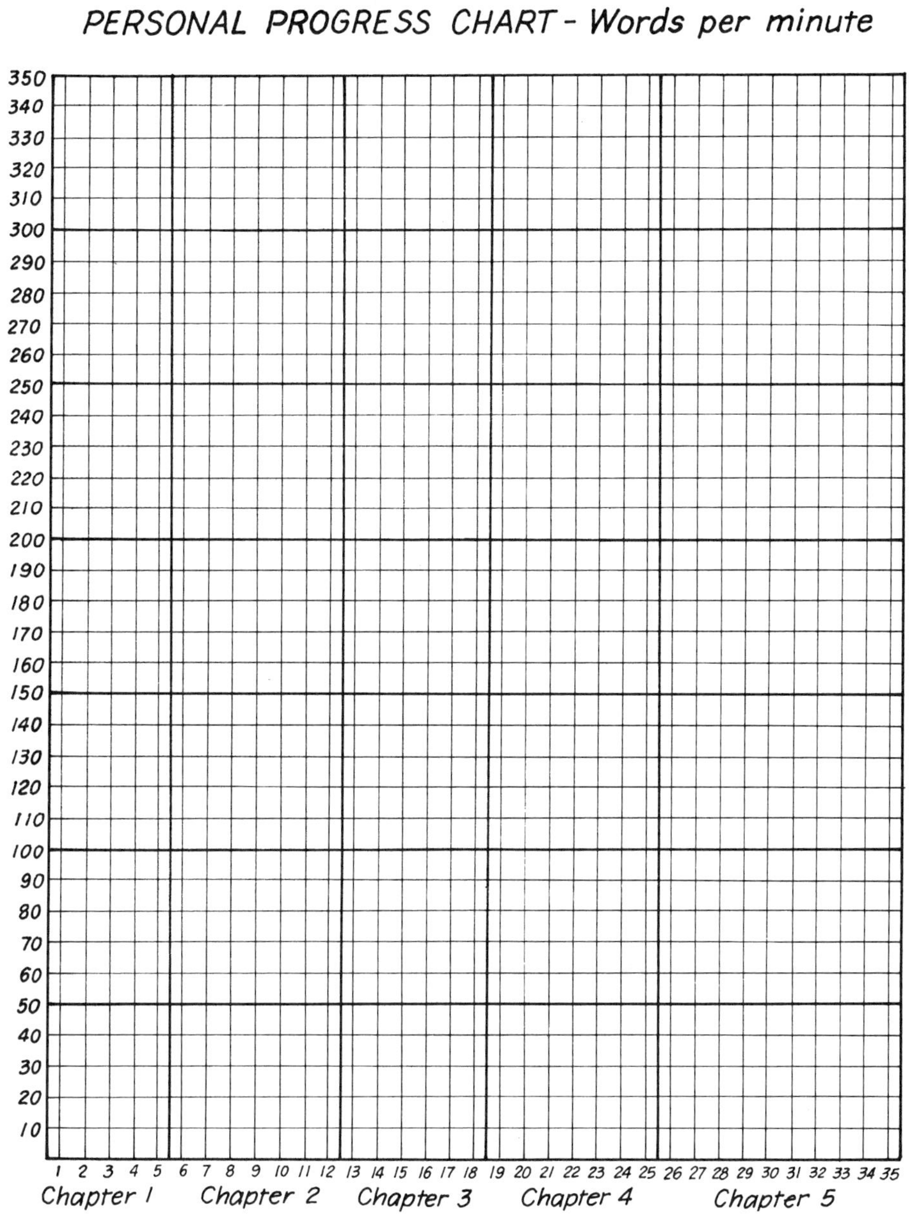

FIGURE 13 PERSONAL PROGRESS CHART - Words per minute

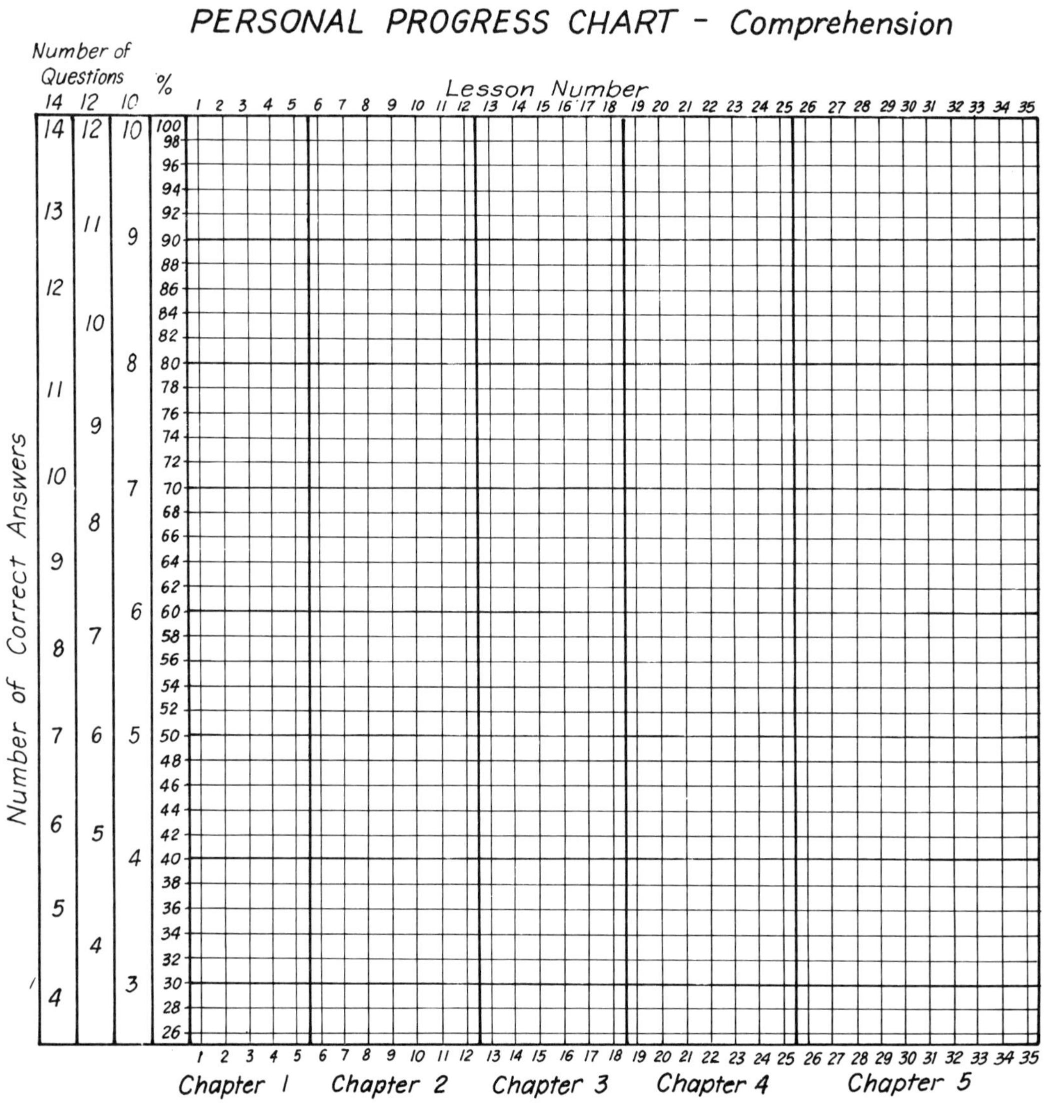

FIGURE 14 PERSONAL PROGRESS CHART – Comprehension

Index